Corinne McNamara

ChildArts
Integrating Curriculum Through the Arts

Jane Schmalholz Garritson

▲ ADDISON-WESLEY PUBLISHING COMPANY

MENLO PARK, CALIFORNIA ○ READING, MASSACHUSETTS ○ LONDON
AMSTERDAM ○ DON MILLS, ONTARIO ○ SYDNEY

This book is in the Addison-Wesley Innovative Series.

Design: Julie Hill

Copyright © 1979 by Addison-Wesley Publishing Company, Inc. All rights reserved. No part of this publication may be reproduced, stored in a retrieval system, or transmitted in any form or by any means, electronic, mechanical, photocopying, recording, or otherwise, without the prior written permission of the publisher. Printed in the United States of America. Published simultaneously in Canada.

CDEFGHIJ–WC–8432

Contents

FOREWORD iv
INTEGRATING CURRICULUM vii

SECTION I
Using an OBJECTIVE INTEREST to integrate art, language arts, drama, science, and ecology   1

MONSTERS 2
- Monster Mini-drama   3
- Monster Dance   5
- Monster Un-Mask   6
- Graph-a-Goblin   8
- Monster Mâché   10
- Adopt-a-Monster   13
- Monster Books   15

CONSTRUCTIONS 16
- Balloon Sculpture   17
- Environmental Construction   20
- Plastic Bag Sculpture   22

SECTION II
Using a CONCEPT to integrate art, math, science, poetry, social studies, and creative writing   25

PATTERN 26
- Pattern Blocks and Quilting   28
- Quilting History   32
  - Language and Follow-Up Activities   34
  - Exhibition Follow-Up   34
- Dip and Dye   35
- Pattern on Pattern   38
- Japanese Accordion Book   40

CAMOUFLAGE 42
- For Animals and Insects   43
- For Kids — Masks   46
- For Teachers — Masks   51
- For Works of Art   53
- For Secret Messages   55

SECTION III.
Using a MATERIAL to integrate art, social studies, math, and science   57

PAPER 58
- Making Paper   59
- Brown Paper Bags and Innertubes   61
- Chop Marks on Paper   64
- Cutting Paper   66
- Equation Necklaces   72
- Wax-Dipped Forms   75
- Papièr-Mâché Fruit and Vegetables   77
- Ozalid Prints   79

SECTION IV
THE PURPOSE OF EDUCATION IN THE ARTS   81
- **About Perceiving**   82
- **About Learning**   84
- **About Additional Benefits of Learning Through the Arts**   88

SECTION V
Using three BASIC TECHNIQUES to integrate art and the child's world   95

DRAWING 96
- Line Drawing   98
- Self Portraits   101
- Contour Drawing   103
- Outdoor Sketching   108
- Drawing Nature   110

PAINTING 113
- Tile Painting   114
- Painting Poems   116
- Painting Found Objects   118

CLAY 121
- Pantomime   22
- Constructions and Impressions   125
- Creatures   128
- Group Sculptures   131
- Clay and Seeds   133

SECTION VI
Using an ELEMENT of art to integrate science and language arts   137

COLOR 138
- Paint a Rainbow   139
- Rainbow Bubbles   141
- Color Variations   143
- Finger Painting   145

SECTION VII
Using an ELEMENT of art to integrate science and language arts   137

MANAGEMENT 149
- Evaluation   150
- Exhibitions   153
- Involving Parents   156

AFTERWORD   159

Foreword

It begins with a few brush strokes then suddenly takes spirited form and comes alive strutting color and exuberance—watching a child describe his world through the medium of paint is one of life's rare privileges. To guide children to express their inner forces and feelings, while nurturing their thoughtful observation and concern for the world around them, is the purpose of this book. The grade level is kindergarten through third grade.

For the very young child, living is a series of experiences that follow one another by accident or caprice rather than by design. Grand discoveries and grand mistakes are made with equal abandon. As the child begins to discriminate, he repeats some activities and avoids others, but he always perceives learning and living as one continuously interacting whole.

The kindergarten child making his first painting will often paint the paper, then the easel, then right up his arm and into real life. He does not yet know there are art surfaces and physical surfaces and social surfaces. He does know that paint is a miracle—the look and smell and feel of it—and that pictures flow effortlessly from the end of his brush. In working with clay, which he pushes and pulls, coils and squishes, he transforms his innermost images into physical shapes that can be touched and shared. Sometimes he sings to the clay for best results. Some times he just pounds and pounds to make it yield.

He loves moving to music with closed eyes, just as he delights in acting out a simple dramatic situation or becoming a familiar storybook character. How do we help him retain this natural sense of joy in expression while we extend his world? How do we develop his sensitivity to appropriate alternatives without fostering a self-conscious attitude about making "art" as something apart from daily concerns?

The child does not consciously set out to create a work of art. He doesn't know or care about such things. He uses art as a way of announcing discoveries and examining his thoughts. He is trying to find out who he is and what he thinks, which is just what the adult artist is doing. The difference between art expression at the elementary level and the creative activity of a great artist is one of degree, not of kind.

The kindergarten child who paints freely will continue to do so into first and second grade if frequent opportunities and specific motivations are provided. Mirrors for self-portraits invite translation of self into line and color. Bringing animals to class to be hugged, handled, and observed will be a major event as long as children and animals exist. Another old standby, the nature walk, is ever successful if accompanied by hands-on exploration, collecting, and talk, talk, talk. A beneficial follow-up is painting or modeling from observation and making collages and prints with the materials gathered on the walk. In this way, each child clarifies and interprets his impressions gained from a real-life situation. The child is not making art as an object removed from his daily concerns—his art is a direct result of them. The child is extending his world, thereby acquiring knowledge and understanding. As a kindergarten child, he cannot adequately express these feelings in written words or sometimes in spoken words, but he can create symbols in his own visual language and communicate, thus experiencing both joy and release from the frustration of verbal communication.

This book is divided into seven sections, five of which present a cluster of activities that integrate art and the other subject areas, analogizing and seeking relationships between them. However, the motivating factor in each one is different.

Section I   is based on the use of two **OBJECTIVE INTERESTS** of children—monsters and constructions.

Section II uses two **CONCEPTS**—pattern and camouflage—to investigate linkage between the arts and math, science, poetry, social studies, and creative writing.

Section III suggests how a **MATERIAL**—paper—can be used to integrate curriculum.

Section V   blends art and the child's world through **BASIC TECHNIQUES**—drawing, painting, and clay.

Section VI connects an **ELEMENT** of art to allied areas of science and language arts.

To formulate written activities is to take a calculated risk. The finest line exists between guided exploration and formula. Although these activities have been thoroughly tested in the classroom, I hope they will function primarily as starters, examples, bases for spin-offs, that they will be enlarged, reduced, or changed to fit the convictions and style of the person presenting them. They should communicate the excitement that comes from thinking in terms of interrelations. Such thinking brings fresh purpose to teaching and learning. These sections begin with an introduction, presenting a rationale for their use. The suggested procedure, the purpose, books, films, materials, new vocabulary words, clues for getting started and, in some cases, proposed extensions are included for each section. Appropriate grade levels are noted but these are generalizations; an open attitude and positive expectations are far better indicators of readiness than is age. A teacher knows his class better than anyone else, just as a parent using this book can judge appropriate materials and direction for his own child.

Section IV is the heart of the book. It discusses the

PURPOSE FOR EDUCATING IN THE ARTS in three articles: "About Perceiving," "About Learning," and "About Additional Benefits of Learning Through the Arts."

Section VII considers many of the questions teachers ask about **MANAGEMENT:** evaluating, exhibiting, and involving parents.

It is not without some soul searching that I use the pronoun "he" throughout the book. Many alternatives were considered—he/she, he or she, and the like. All are unwieldy; hence, we chose the least obtrusive usage.

I wish to thank Bradwell Scott, Barbara and Christopher Wagstaff, and Helen Bacon for constructive suggestions; my family—Paul, Darian, and Kip—for their ever-present support and encouragement; and my silent partners—all the children with whom I have worked.

Integrating Curriculum

Why integrate curriculum? There are several reasons. The preschool child approaches living and learning as one inseparable whole. Then he goes to school and often finds science, math, language arts, social studies, and the arts taught as entirely separate entities. Each is presented as an end in itself although the essence of daily living is their constant interchange. The child may come to regard the subject areas, when presented in 40-minute modules, as unnatural and so far removed from each other and from his own involvements that he is unable to connect what he learns in school with his needs and activities outside school. He begins to separate school (learning) from the real world (living). This schism widens with time and by high school, unable to handle both, he may opt for the real world and drop out.

Isn't it true that, as we mature, our experience, with increasing consistency, reveals threads of relatedness? We're reminded of similarities, metaphors, analogies. They shrink our world and make it more manageable. Fortunately, we have these to call on when faced with what at first appears new and unfamiliar—they help us to proceed rather than be overwhelmed. Making sense of the world is much easier for the child who has been helped to see that new things he must learn contain at least fragments of something he already knows, that learning means relating and combining, not separating.

Creating situations for discovering relationships between content areas, pushing the areas to overlap as they do in life, brings an excitement to learning. For instance, basic reading may well be taught in a focused 40-minute module, giving precedence to reading processes and skills development. But reading should be given a broader context regularly during these periods, by relating the skills being learned to activities in the arts and other subject areas. If these activities are important to the student, and if reading and careful observation are necessary components for participation, then learning to read takes on new meaning through immediate purpose.

Bruno Bettelheim in *The Uses of Enchantment* says, "I have become deeply dissatisfied with much of the literature intended to develop the child's mind and personality because the pre-primers and primers from which he is taught to read in school are designed to teach the necessary skills, irrespective of meaning. The acquisition of skills, including the ability to read, becomes devalued when what one has learned to read adds nothing of importance to one's life."

Integrating curriculum by blurring the harder edges of the disciplines and revealing ideas common to all need not violate the integrity of language arts, math, the arts, science or social studies, nor make them less than they are. On the contrary, encouraging a child to think in terms of their relatedness increases their value and gives him a sense of an underlying unity of experience, purpose, and process, of which he is a part.

SECTION I

Using an OBJECTIVE INTEREST to integrate art, language arts, drama, science, and ecology

MONSTERS

Monsters conjure up an infinite variety of images and encourage the free play of whimsical imagination. Since every monster is possible and every representation "right," every child is successful. Monsters can be an attractive stratagem for involving students in social studies, science, language arts, math, body movement, music, and art as well as for investigating relationships between these content areas.

Actually becoming a monster is relatively easy for the most hesitant child because the characteristics are so exaggerated. Qualities such as wildness or terror or hilarity, which are eminently understandable because they border on caricature, are easier for children and adults to act out than subtler shadings of these traits like restlessness, dismay, or mild amusement. Similarly, imitating an animal like a monkey with long swinging arm movements, crouched position, and bent-knee walk is easier than portraying a fawn, which has no clearly identifiable characteristics that lend themselves easily to caricature.

You can begin a series of explorations for young children by reading aloud one of the creature books like *The Monster's Nose Was Cold*, by Joan Hanson or *Where the Wild Things Are*, by Maurice Sendakm. As you read, become each character; use a few props. If you are reading *Wild Things*, take time to cut a couple of big ears from construction paper, staple them to a 2-inch paper band to fit your head, and wear it. An old pair of garden gloves with 4-inch long, thin red paper "nails" pinned to each finger as claws plus a piece of rope tied around your waist and hanging tail-like in back will delight the class. These props are quickly made into visual suggestions. Young children supply all the imagination needed to accept such objects as part of the fantasy. They are sure to insist that you read the story several times—let them join in by supplying growls at the proper places. It develops their listening faculties.

When the story is finished, take advantage of their childlike desires to portray monsters by moving them into characterization as described in the procedure for Monster Drama. The child, then, in focusing on his interpretation of monster qualities, begins to transform his natural sense of play into controlled communication. Movement and mime set the stage for the Monster Dance. Then Monster Un-Masks add a convincing prop for students to use. Invite them to repeat the Monster Dance, this time wearing the masks.

Graph-a-Goblin is a group activity requiring less movement and more concentration. Monster Mâché, another group activity, requires an hour or so commitment each day for a couple of weeks. Part of people's fascination with papier-mâché is watching it take shape over a period of time.

Adopt-a-Monster is a final wrap-up in which a number of questions about monsters can be put to rest.

For mature second- and third-graders, consider the books listed in the bibliography at the end of the section. Many include photographs and drawings, in many cases of real animals, that are sure to pique interest and stimulate inquiry.

Just a word about the occasional child who is genuinely frightened by even benign monsters and does not want to participate. Having him act as monitor, passing out paper, starting the record for the monster dance, in short, assisting the teacher, and then observing the proceedings as spectator rather than participant should prove less threatening. Coming to see monsters as just cardboard and make-believe instead of actual beings is easier for him from this vantage point.

Monster Mini-Drama

MATERIALS
> None

BOOKS
> Viola Spolin, *Improvisation for the Theater*, Chapter 15, "Workshop for Six- to Eight-Year-Olds" (Northwestern University Press).
> Geraldine Brain Siks, *Creative Dramatics* (Harper & Row).
> Geraldine Brain Siks, *Drama with Children* (Harper & Row).

INTERRELATING
> Language arts through vocabulary extension
> Physical education through controlled body movements

PURPOSE
> Develop free play of imaginative ideas
> Communicate and share these ideas
> Build vocabulary
> Express ideas through controlled body movements

PROCEDURE (K–1)

Starting with questioning strategies gives the child a few simple clues to which he can respond. This helps establish confidence and freedom for testing his own imagination, for example:

HOW DOES A MONSTER MOVE? DOES HE PROWL? HOP? SNEAK? JUMP? CRAWL? SKIP? DOES HE WALK ON ALL FOURS? SHOW ME. (Good playground activity.)

Get everyone into a monster's skin. If you use the center of the room, avoid children's irresistible temp-

tation to touch and punch, which accompanies such free movement and fantasizing, by having them s—t—r—e—t—c—h their arms out to the side, turn in a circle, and clear their own areas before proceeding.

MINI-DRAMA

Again, start the action with questions:

NOW, PRETEND YOU ARE A MONSTER JUST GETTING UP IN THE MORNING. HOW DO YOU WASH YOUR FACE, MONSTER? COMB YOUR HAIR? (IT'S DOWN TO YOUR KNEES, MONSTER.) HOW DO YOU BRUSH YOUR TEETH? TOOTH? HOW MANY DO YOU HAVE? HOW LONG ARE THEY, MONSTER?

By imitating familiar everyday activities and thinking and talking about them simultaneously, children can clarify and refine their movements and gestures during the act of interpretation.

WHAT KINDS OF SOUNDS DO YOU MAKE, MONSTER? DO YOU WHISTLE? GARGLE? SNORT? GROWL? ROAR? GIGGLE?

Children build vocabulary with constant questioning. If you have single word concepts you wish to develop, set up such a situation to accommodate them, for example:

LET ME HEAR A HIGH SOUND YOUR MONSTER CAN MAKE. Have them use their hands to describe "high." LET ME HEAR A LOW SOUND. Use hands again. Continual references of this kind will prepare them for the concept of high and low notes when you teach music. When the children begin to get the feel of mime and movement, it is time for the Monster Dance.

Monster Dance

MATERIALS
None

BOOKS
Gilliom, *Basic Movement Education for Children: Rationale and Teaching Units* (Addison-Wesley).
Dimondstein, *Exploring the Arts with Children* (Macmillan).

INTERRELATING
Body movement through coordination
Music through rhythm

PURPOSE
Feel a relationship between body movement and various rhythms
Orchestrate music, movement, and verbal directions for body control and enjoyment

PROCEDURE (K – 1)

Body movements seem easier and flow more naturally when set to music. You need a record with a lively beat but not too fast, and a small tom-tom or drum. Beat the rhythm for them.

Again, work in the center of the room, spaced out, letting body movements take over. Feel the music. Suggest they close their eyes and let the music move them. Tap the beat. Occasionally alternate with a slower record. Tap the beat—it develops coordination and body control.

Find excuses to move to music often. If the center of the room is not available, then parade around the outside or between the desks. Set the cadance with record and drum. As they move along, sing out suggestions like:

March March with hands on head —let them move 25 steps then
March March with hands on hips —let them move 25 steps then
March March clap on the beat —let them move 25 more steps

Make up a whole series of postures. With practice they will learn to perform two movements at once in rhythm without breaking stride. Very good for coordination.

Monster Un-Mask

MATERIALS
- Tagboard or scrap cardboard approximately 12" x 18"
- Crayons
- Felt-tip pens
- Elmer's glue, glue sticks, or paste
- Stapler
- Light-weight found objects

BOOKS
- Alkema, *Monster Masks* (Sterling).
- Mayer, *Little Monster Word Book* (Golden Press).

INTERRELATING
- Language arts through vocabulary extension and oral communication of ideas and fantasy images

PURPOSE
- Interpret verbal descriptions through visual forms
- Share fantasy images through oral descriptions
- Choose and compose a variety of materials to express an idea
- Experiment with attaching and connecting various materials and objects
- Expand vocabulary
- Develop painting and drawing skills

PROCEDURE (K–1)

Young children love wearing masks almost as much as wearing hats. An easy and practical mask can be made by cutting an oval face-shaped hole, approximately child-size, in 12"x18" tag-board or a large piece of recycled cardboard. The teacher cuts the holes if the children are too young to manage scissors. The child projects his face through the hole and can decorate the remaining board space with colored crayon, felt-tip pen, cut and paste decoration, and light-weight found objects. Some masks, such as paper bag masks, make seeing and moving difficult—these un-masks solve both problems.

With face holes cut, the children are now ready to create their own monsters. Prime their imaginations with some questions: IS YOUR MONSTER FURRY, CURLY OR FUZZY? DOES HE HAVE EARS? ROUND OR POINTED? BIG OR LITTLE? HAIRY OR SMOOTH? Keep a conversation going with the students while they are drawing, painting and decorating. DOES YOUR MONSTER HAVE HORNS? HOW MANY? Encourage their opinions and statements and accept them all. The children will incorporate into the masks individual interpretations of these verbalized suggestions through form, line and color. Their vocabulary will grow and act as motivation by providing a flow of alternatives. The input is all child-oriented. They are sharing ideas, supporting each other, and developing. With so many possibilities, fewer children will say, "I can't draw ears" (or horns or whatever). Keep them too busy talking and drawing to consider any thought of inadequacy.

If they are cutting and pasting, show them how to fringe hair and curl strips around a pencil as illustrated. Then paste them on the mask. If these additions hang down over the cut-out face space, so much the better—peeking through paper curls adds to the frolic.

Staple two paper strips to the back of the masks as shown in the picture to assure a comfortable fit. This un-mask will survive much activity.

For an optional extension, have the children put their un-masks on and paint colored shapes on their own faces with water soluble felt-tip pens. If you anticipate any parental objection, send home a ditto explaining the program for, say, Monster Wednesday. Invite the parents and any younger children to help and perhaps paint their faces, too. There is something magical about it for all ages.

If the children respond to this activity with enthusiasm you may wish to have them make monster wrist- or ankle-bands to wear with the masks. Decorate strips of colored paper cut 3" wide, then staple them on the wrists and/or ankles. By this time the children will feel free enough to try a number of things. They can experiment with taping found objects to the bands. This is good practice. If it does not go on right, they can color over the masking tape with felt-tips or crayons. They can pull pieces of yarn through holes punched in the paper and tie objects on the ends. This entire activity is excellent for encouraging free choice of materials and gets them to invent new ways of attaching and connecting.

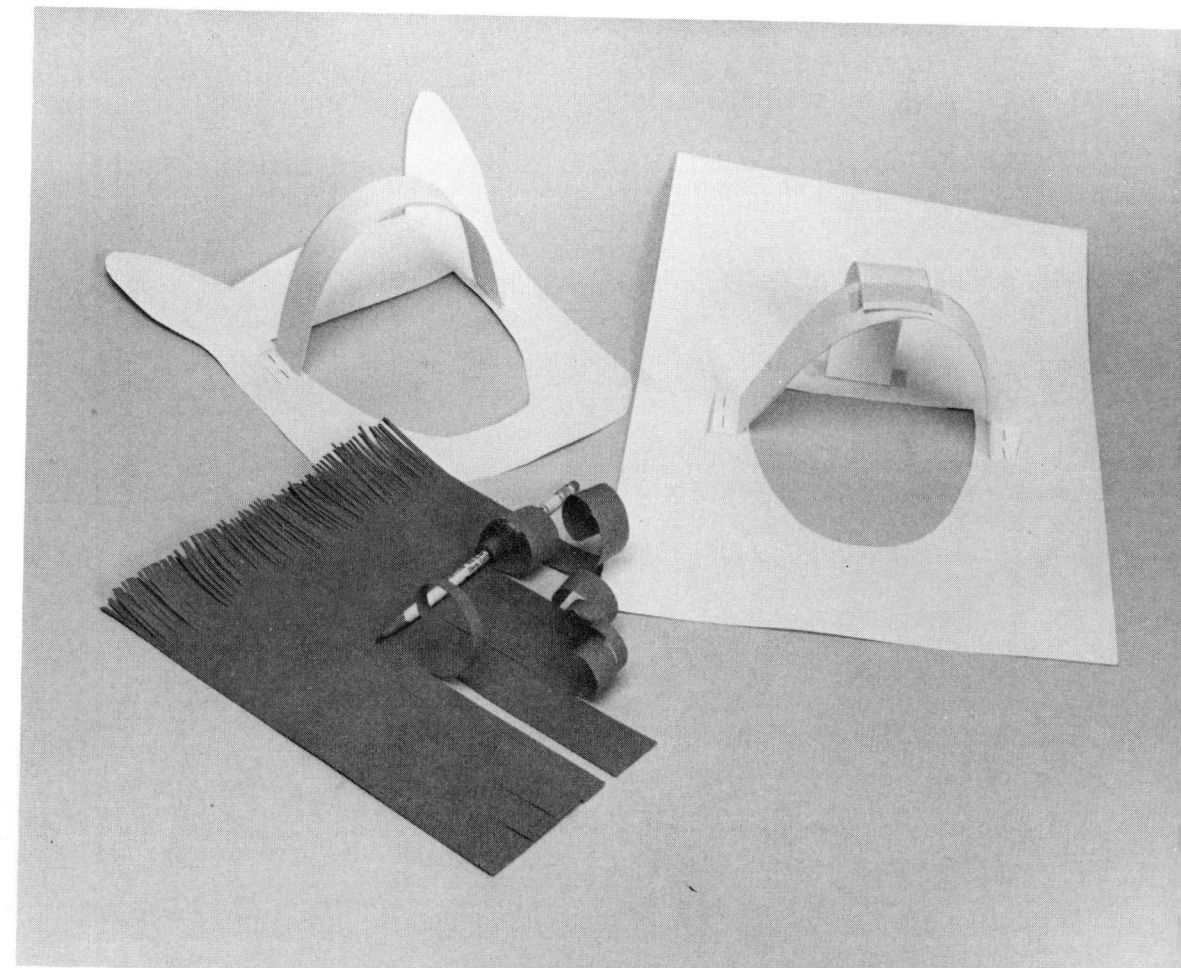

Graph-a-Goblin

MATERIALS
    Butcher paper, 12" × 18" newsprint, or drawing paper
    Pins or tape for assembling
    Scissors
    Paint, crayons, or felt-tip pens

BOOKS
    Viorst, *My Mama Says There Aren't Any Zombies Ghosts Vampires Creatures Demons Monsters Fiends Goblins or Things* (Atheneum).
    Wallace, *Monster Poems* (Holiday).
    Mayer, *One Monster After Another* (Golden Press).
    Delaney, *One Dragon to Another* (Houghton Mifflin).

PURPOSE
    Observe body parts and how they fit together
    Examine the relationship of beings with their environment
    Practice inventing and fabricating images

PROCEDURE (K–1)

Because a goblin does not have a standard image, as does a witch, invention is the basic ingredient in creating a good goblin. Distribute pieces of butcher paper or newsprint and have each child draw a goblin part, using one medium—paint, crayons, or felt-tip pens—for visual consistency. This time the game is "fill the page with a part." One child might draw a head with horns, a second huge eyes, several feet or paws, and another a long, long tail. You may have to specify some parts for proper distribution. Have them cut out the completed part. Even if not perfect, it is quite acceptable for a goblin, and good practice with scissors. Next, supply a large butcher-paper body (3' × 5' or 6'), free-form in shape. Tack it on the wall at child-height and let each child add his part to the body. This requires considering the placement of leg, arm, neck (some don't even know about necks yet and won't unless you talk about them and help them look for and find them), head, fingers, nostrils, and nails. Using themselves and each other to observe connections is an easy way to learn.

See what kind of goblin you come up with. Name him or her. WHERE MIGHT HE LIVE? CAN HE GET IN A HOLE IN THE GROUND? WOULD HE PREFER A NEST IN A TREE OR A BRICK HOUSE? WHAT ABOUT A CAVE? After this discussion is a good time to initiate a drawing. Draw the goblin you have created and show him in his home. WHAT IS THE GOBLIN'S FAIMLY LIKE? ANY SISTERS? BROTHERS? WHAT KIND OF SCHOOL DOES HE GO TO? WHAT KIND OF DESKS DO GOBLINS USE? Second-graders might consider what goblins eat and each write a grocery list from a goblin's point of reference. HOW WOULD YOU ENTERTAIN A GOBLIN IF HE CAME TO VISIT YOU—TAKE HIM TO THE MOVIES? COULD HE SLEEP IN YOUR BED? WHAT BOOK WOULD THE CLASS READ TO HIM?

With this background of information and examination, a papier-mâché goblin-monster should come rather easily.

Monster Mâché

MATERIALS
    Newspaper
    Wallpaper paster (available at your hardware store, inexpensive)
    String
    Dishpan
    Recycled latex paint and powdered tempera
    Painter's plastic drop cloth or scrap plastic (optional)
    Shellac (optional)

BOOKS
    J. and C. Kenny, *Design in Papier Mâché* (Chilton).
    McLaughlin, *Papier Mâché* (Larousse & Co.).
    Betts, *Exploring Papier Mâché* (Davis).
    Meilach, *Papier Mâché* (Crown Publishing).
    Johnson, *Papier Mâché* (David McKay & Co.).

PURPOSE
    Learn to cooperate in a group activity
    Work through a process requiring sequencing
    Watch a form develop over a time period
    Appreciate the work involved in a large project

NEW VOCABULARY
    core   latex paint
    layering   feathered edge
    stripping

The lumpier, nubbier, and more mis-shapen a goblin monster grows, the better—perfect foil for papier-mâché. Most children love working in this medium. It is messy, but therein lie its charm and attraction. A large monster—children are fascinated by making something "big"—can be made in spring, outside in the grass where they can work freely and a few pasty drips will go unnoticed. Besides, it will dry faster outside. If there is no grass, use a plastic painter's drop cloth or a large piece of scrap plastic.

Working in large scale makes a good group project. Four students can work at one time, until everyone gets a turn. Then begin again.

The body can easily be made by crushing newspapers into a shape, wrapping it with string, then continuing the process until the body size is right. It should be fairly solid. All appendages can be made with the same kind of newspaper core and attached with string. This core will be covered so don't worry about its appearance. Do connect all parts well. After the first three layers of mâché, the parts will firm up and hold in place.

After the rough framework, or core, is ready the layering can begin. Mix wallpaper paste and water to the consistency of thin cream, in a dishpan. Have the children tear newspaper in 2" strips. It is easier for them to tear straight along the length of the page with the grain. Well, almost straight. This is a good coordination practice. The feathered edges will blend into each other when pasted;

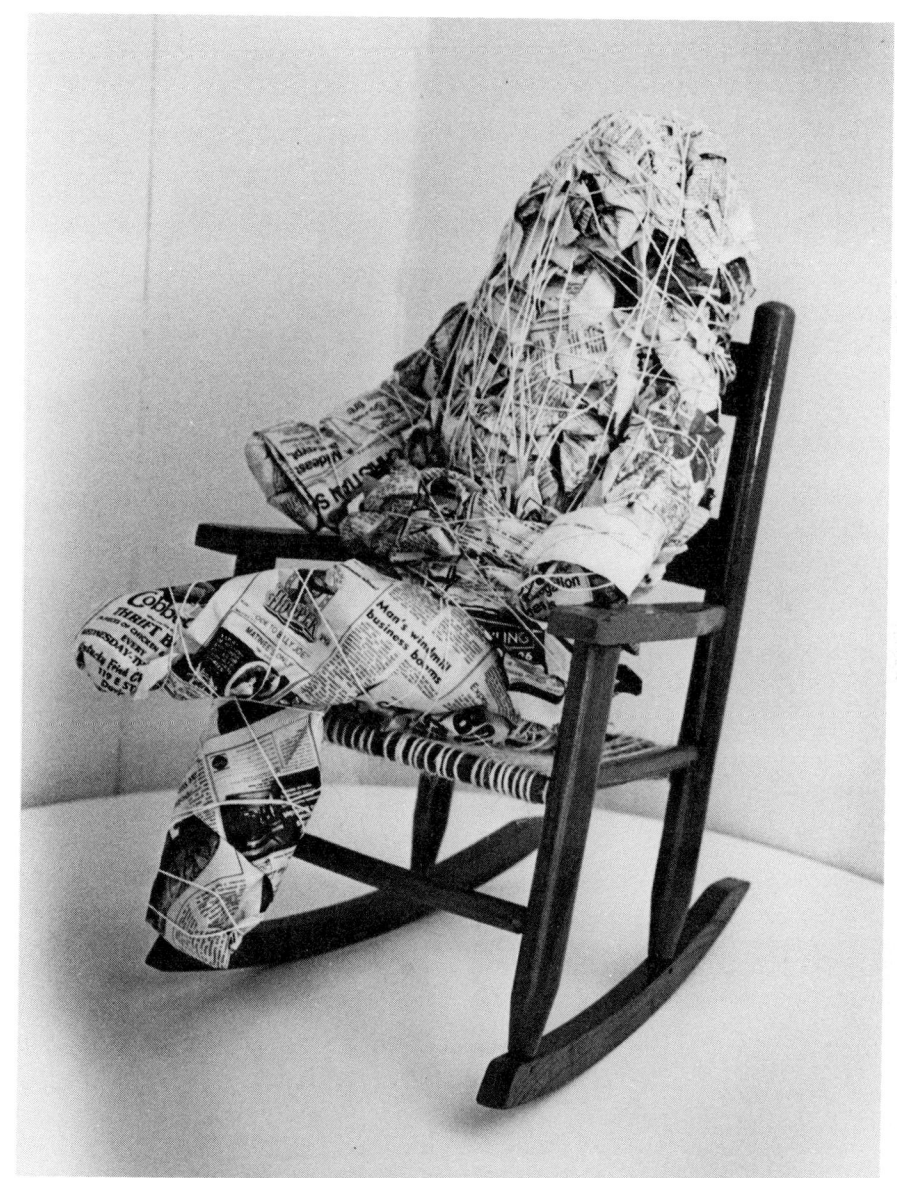

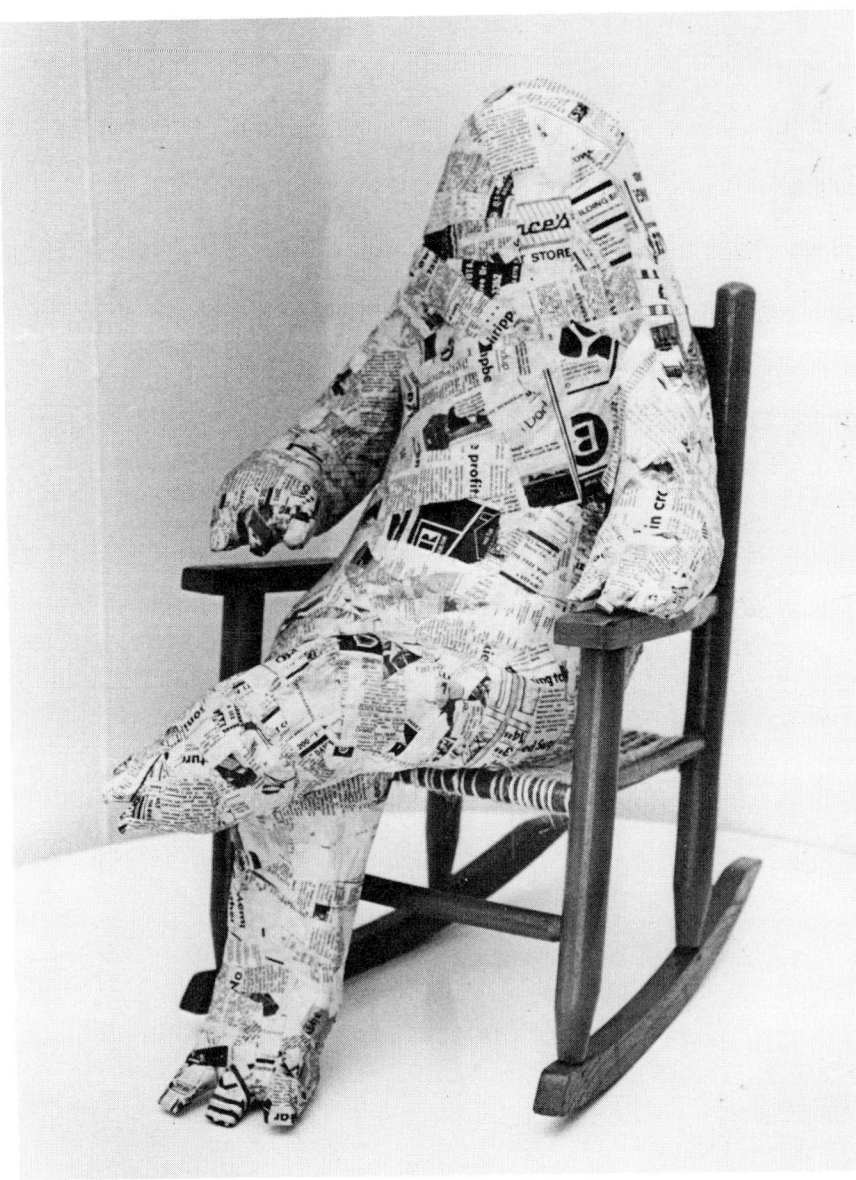

however, if the strips are cut with scissors the hard edges can never be concealed.

Dip the strips in the paste mixture, then hold them with one hand and pull between the thumb and forefinger of the other to remove the excess paste. Hold the strips over the dishpan to catch the dripping mixture. Apply strips overlapping each other, in all directions for strength, until the exposed surface of the monster core is covered. No more than three layers should be applied each day because drying between sessions is necessary. If a surface area gets too wet it will collapse. Explain to the children that they should work over the entire body. Cover any holes that appear; rotate the shape daily so all sides are covered. Five to eight layers make a super-strong shape. An easy way to track the number of layers and distribute the strips evenly is to use black and white newsprint for the first layer, the green section for the second, and brown paper bag strips for the third, for strength. Repeat the black and white for the fourth and finish with green sheets or paper toweling for a really fine last layer.

When the monster is dry, give it a flat coat of latex paint. The finishing coat of paint, and the eyes, ears, hair and mouth should now go on. For information about mixing paint, see page 119. If details are painted on with straight tempera, a final overall coat of shellac or varnish, sprayed or brushed, is a practical idea. Such a mâché monster will hold up for several years of spirited treatment from children.

Adopt-a-Monster

MATERIALS
    Recycled paper bags, tuna cans, small boxes, glass jars
    Aluminum foil
    Natural materials: leaves, twigs, small rocks

BOOKS
    Gross and Railton, *Teaching Science in an Outdoor Environment* (University of California Press, 1972).
    Lund, *I Wonder What's Under* (Parents, 1970).

INTERRELATING
    Natural science through exploration of creature environments and of their purposes

PURPOSE
    Distinguish between real creatures and fantasy monsters
    Extend appreciation of living things
    Identify some needs of these other living things

NEW VOCABULARY
    balance of nature

PROCEDURE (K-2)

Are there really such things as monsters or do we make them up? A discussion of just what makes a monster could be helpful in clearing up children's misapprehensions and vague fears. Does size have something to do with making a monster? Would the group goblin have been as monstrous if he had been smaller? Do we think of a dog as a monster? Does a cat? Do we think of a cat as a monster? Does a mouse?

When you take your nature walk look for some creepy-crawlies. The children, working in pairs, can find a spider, snail, worm, or who-knows-what to bring back for observation. If preferred, examine and discuss the creatures on the spot. Each pair will need a small box or tuna can. HOW WOULD YOU MAKE A HOME FOR THIS CREATURE? CAN IT LIVE IN THE BOX OR A PIECE OF ALUMINUM FOIL? Talk about the size. DOES THE CREATURE NEED TO MOVE AROUND? This might govern selection of the container. (Might protective natural covering like a leaf or a few twigs make the creature more comfortable?) A glass jar allows the children to see the underside of snails or other invertebrates as they crawl. WHAT DOES IT EAT? WHAT ABOUT WATER? Working in pairs with one creature can help stimulate students' conversation and exchange of ideas.

Discuss with them what the creature is good for, if he has a particular job to do, if he helps maintain nature's balance.

Whether a creature becomes a "monster" depends on our point of view.

Closure for this project might involve a ceremony of returning the creatures to their natural surroundings. The children should understand that *every* animal and insect has a place and is needed there, just like each one of us.

MONSTER BOOKS

Soule, *The Mystery Monsters* (Putnam).
> A book of salient facts and guesses man has amassed to date about mysterious creatures that do or may inhabit planet Earth. For older children. Illustrated with photographs.

Soule, *The Maybe Monsters* (Putnam).
> Some have been proven to exist, others, such as the Abominable Snowman and Loch Ness monster, are maybe monsters. Few illustrations, many photographs. For older children.

McHargue, *The Beasts of Never* (Bobbs Merrill).
> A book about imaginary creatures. Some are familiar—dragon, unicorn, sea serpent—others are less well known—hippogriff, roc, Amphisbaena.

Wise, *Monsters of the Ancient Seas* (Putnam).
> Exotic creatures from ancient oceans. Many illustrations. For younger children.

Williams and Mayer, *Everyone Knows What a Dragon Looks Like* (Four Winds/Scholastic).
> Breathtaking illustrations.

Flora and McElderry, *The Great Green Turkey Creek Monster* (Atheneum).

Wise, *Monsters of Today and Yesterday* (Putnam).
> Exploration into the world of unique but real animals, past and present. Line drawings. For young readers.

Blance, et al., *Monster Series* (Bowmar Publishing Corp., 1973). Available in English and Spanish.
> *Monster Comes to the City*
> *Monster Meets a Lady Monster*
> *Monster Has a Party*
> *Monster at School*

CONSTRUCTIONS

Children are curious about how things go together. Exercises through which children can experiment and learn—first-hand—how to build, what kind of connecting material to use, and a bit about stresses and tolerances are important because some children never see repair or construction work in their homes. They will likely grow up with only vague ideas of how things work without exposure to structuring and to the fine art of tinkering. The following construction-sculpture activities are small beginnings designed to initiate students into the thought processes behind assemblage while teaching them about pattern, color, texture, and spatial elements.

It has been said that new discoveries in materials and connecting techniques lead to new forms. In architecture, the invention of steel lead to the skyscraper; and stressed concrete lead to the extended cantilever, the geodesic dome, and to economically spanning vast areas. New materials and connectors allow us to think new thoughts about what is possible; first, however, it is logical to understand what we already have at hand.

Balloon Sculpture requires rubber cement rather than Elmer's glue because of the rubber surface. Connecting round shapes is quite different in practice and result from working with flat shapes. Tying, as in the Plastic Bag Sculpture, is a form of connecting used since earliest times. It is easy for children to handle and allows for experimentation and frequent reorganization as better ideas occur.

The activities are sequenced in order of difficulty: Balloon Sculpture, Environmental Construction, and last, Plastic Bag Sculpture. However, any one may be presented out of sequence depending on the class ability and experience.

Balloon Sculpture

MATERIALS
  Balloons in assorted colors
  Rubber cement
  Tempera paint
  Felt-tip pens in colors
  Rubber bands

BOOKS
  Lamorisse, *The Red Balloon* (Doubleday).
  Stone, *Balloon People* (McGraw-Hill).
  Hunt, ed., *Balloons Are* (Holt, Rinehart and Winston).
  G. Timmermans, *The Great Balloon Race* (Addison-Wesley)

PURPOSE
  Make judgments
  Experience the process of constructing, considering physical and visual requirements
  Improvising during a process to accommodate new ideas
  Sharing, compromising, and working in a group

NEW VOCABULARY
  rubber cement
  sculpture
  space
  gently

PROCEDURE (1-3)

Kids love balloons. That's the way it's supposed to be. Adults love balloons because they're reminded of

childhood pleasures, so making sculptures with balloons is a playful venture for both child and adult.

The material is familiar. If one balloon is a beautiful round bauble, think how seven or nine or twelve, connected and painted with tempera, will look. Fifteen to twenty balloons (they are not expensive) are adequate for a group of three or four children—five to seven or more for an individual child.

The connecting material is rubber cement. After the balloons are blown up, take one and gently paint a spot of cement about the size of a silver dollar anywhere on the surface. Then hold a second balloon against this spot. Fortunately for youthful interest and patience, it will bond almost immediately. Anyone can paste balloons together randomly, but this activity provides an opportunity to combine them in such a way that they project into space and tell us about themselves, arousing speculations and feelings, thus becoming sculpture. Painting has one face, being two-dimensional, but a three-dimensional sculpture has many so it is necessary to consider all these faces during development instead of just working on the front view. Remind the students to move around the construction when adding balloons, to look at it from many angles. You may have to remind them a number of times because they are accustomed to drawing, painting, and collage—none of which involves the third dimension of space.

Many children prefer making a boat, flag, flower, or hot rod for their first balloon sculpture. It gives them a place to start and the security of a concrete object. As they work, talk about the possibility of their object turning into something else. If this hot rod wants to turn into a snail, they can let it do so. The students need to know this is acceptable. This metamorphosis type of activity more likely will take place if the students are working in groups. There is usually one maverick who will kid around and comment that the seven-balloon-daisy looks more like a bee trying to become a butterfly. Take advantage of such observations. Encourage the students to step back occasionally and look at what they have done. Suggest that they turn their cluster of balloons upside down or sideways and observe the new form. What do they see? Do they prefer this arrangement? Sometimes the flow of material and circumstances takes them in a different direction from their first intentions. Of course nothing is wrong with following an idea through to its finish, but moving beyond the execution of a preconceived idea should also be encouraged.

Painting the balloon sculpture with tempera, flow pen lines, and/or colored shapes is a further extension of the organizing and combining phase. Often a descriptive line or shape helps clarify the intent of the work and visually connect the rounds.

The key word in working with balloons is "gently" —blow, connect, and build gently. Children will pop them at first but that passes when the sculptures begin to develop and it becomes more important to use the balloons for additional shapes than to pop them for effect or because of carelessness. After the sculptures have been completed, observed, and commented on by the class, try combining two or more, with the creators' consent of course, for dramatic effect. Suspend the sculpture from the ceiling. The children should not be disappointed if some balloons have shrivelled and lost their shape by the second day because the value of the activity is in the making and sharing.

Another approach to working with balloons is to have each student create a flying machine, a space ship, an underwater vessel, or any other suggestion you or the class can come up with simply by building the balloon into a construction of colored or painted paper. These can also be hung (see illustrations).

Environmental Construction

MATERIALS
    Small objects to be brought in by the students
    Several large boxes from the supermarket
    Odds and ends of materials—Styrofoam trays, string, buttons, ribbon, wire, colored paper, cardboard scraps, etc.
    Glue—Elmer's or any other kind in the classroom

BOOKS
    Skelsey and Huckaby, *Growing Up Green* (Workman Publishing Co.).
    Gross and Railton, *Teaching Science in an Outdoor Environment* (University of California Press).

PURPOSE
    Examine the meaning of environment
    Define the importance of our environment to our lives
    Generate and select ideas
    Verbalize and explain a process

NEW VOCABULARY
    ecology
    environment
    smog

PROCEDURE (2–3)

    We talk a lot now about environment, about its meaning and its influence. Students in the elementary grades need some first-hand experience in dealing with the concept.

There is a mental environment. Can it influence our thinking, lift our spirits, develop our confidence? There is a physical environment. Can it influence our well-being? Should it be country or city living? Are crowded conditions detrimental? We know smog is bad, but which is preferable—warm or cool climates? Should we live in the ground or on top of it, in the air or in the water? How do we protect the environment in order to raise enough food for all? Does color in our surroundings affect our behavior? This activity is designed to stimulate the students to think about such questions and to generate more of their own.

Have each student bring in a small object that he finds intriguing. It may be mineral, vegetable, or simulated animal. Set up a display table and allow a week or so for the students to get into the spirit of the project. See who can bring in the most controversial object, the most beautiful, the most obscure, or the most unique one from the beach, mountains or kitchen. When there are enough objects to supply one for each child, or in a group activity, enough for several groups, the work can begin. Give each child or group a box of appropriate size to accommodate the object plus elbow room with breathing space around it. The idea is to build (in the box) an environment in which this object can thrive. These conditions and surroundings may incorporate drawing, painting, cut paper, found objects, suspended or projected shapes glues, taped or laced to the box. You may wish to specify either fantasy or representational environments as equally acceptable. The purpose is to get the students to think in terms of the most beneficial situation for this "thing."

The students, working in groups, begin by talking about the object. This gives them practice verbalizing and playing off each other's ideas. The more odd the object (it may be just a shape with no identifiable use), the more conversation will be generated. Get them to look carefully at their object, talk about its qualities, its future, its past, and to speculate, hypothesize, project, and infer. These suggestions might be tabulated by the scribe in the group or by the students in a round-robin letter. Then put the letter away and read it after the box-environment is completed to compare how it all began with how it ended.

This is another of those times to bring out all the odds and ends you have saving for manipulative projects: Styrofoam trays, string, buttons, ribbon, toothpicks, etcetera. Most teachers know this list by heart and have saved this kind of thing for years. Natural materials—leaves, twigs, rocks, and the like—can also be added.

The box itself may be placed so that one must look down into it or it may rest on a side. In this position, the environmental construction will take on the appearance of a diorama. Suggest painting or pasting colored paper on the inside walls to create the appearance of earth, sky, water, space. This sets the stage for the action. It is a good idea for the students to play around with shapes, locations, colors, and relationships within the box before final gluing. Time is needed to generate and select ideas. The discussion period at the beginning is very important and should not be rushed. Each group should be given a few minutes after completing its project to talk about it. If the activity is on an individual basis, each child can write a short paragraph or explanation to accompany his presentation. You can learn a great deal about the students' conception and understanding of environment by listening to their conversation during the course of the project.

Plastic Bag Sculpture

MATERIALS
    Plastic bags from the supermarket produce section
    Colored paper
    Recycled cottage cheese cartons, Styrofoam cups, milk cartons, margarine tubs, Styrofoam packing, etc.
    Newspaper
    Leaves, feathers, all sorts of textured materials
    String
    Old screen wire or hardware cloth
    Reclaimed pieces of wood—broom handles, short planks, and the like

BOOKS (General Construction)
    Lincoln and Torry, *A Workshop of Your Own* (Houghton Mifflin).
    Sharp, *Simple Machines and How They Work* (Random House).
    Wyler and Ames, *What Makes It Go?* (McGraw-Hill).

PURPOSE
    Develop the ability to innovate—making choices and evaluating
    Extend tactile-visual sense
    Experience the value of patterning
    Use familiar materials in new and strange ways
    Explore the concepts of piling, layering, stacking, and grouping with actual material

PROCEDURE (2-3)

An inexpensive material for construction-sculpture, a material that is light and easily manipulated by children, is hard to come by. However, there is one resource we have in abundance—the plastic bags available in the produce section of most groceries and supermarkets. They can be stuffed with cut paper in an array of colors, with cardboard shapes (circular bands, triangles, or ready-mades), decorated boxes, cottage cheese containers or their tops stripped with colored paper, or decorated milk cartons cut in surprising ways. The bags can also be filled with shredded newspaper, closed, and laced with string to create simple shapes. Even the colored printed matter on the bag can become part of the overall design. The number and variety of inventive possibilities is endless. The class will have many suggestions.

Send a note home asking that all these plastic bags be saved and sent to school. In addition, smaller sandwich bags add a variety in size.

The stuffed bags are assembled into patterns determined by their filling—whether by color, style of cutting, shape of objects, size of bag—then tied to a large piece of recycled screenwire or hardward cloth to form a solid surface. The wire or metal cloth may be mounted flat against a wall or, more exciting, formed into a shape and covered with these bags.

Another construction might take a form determined by a reclaimed broom handle or long piece of wood, covered in some fashion and hung from the ceiling with the bags. Other stuffed bags can be suspended from this basic bar, simulating giant fringe. By substituting wire for string, you open a whole new range of possibilities because the wire can be bent into directed projections and shapes. This is the kind of open and free construction that invites experimentation. Because the material is not precious or costly, changes are easily performed and any idea can be considered. Some children may want to make a recognizable object while others will feel free to investigate piling, layering, stacking, or grouping, in terms of color, texture, shape, space, or pattern. As the construction grows, repetition of size, color, or texture—perhaps all three—will exert a unifying influence and the students can begin to recognize, even in a small way, the importance of pattern and repetition as a synthesizing element.

The adult artist, when working with materials allowing the freedom this project permits, often finds himself alternating between periods of vigorous production accompanied by torrents of ideas and stretches of trial and error that slow his progress. Therefore, this kind of creative investigation requires frequent comment and encouragement from the teacher to bridge the periods of uncertainty. Questioning strategies can also be used to advantage here. Direct questioning of the group (this project lends itself to group activity) about their current ideas, direction, and expectations requires their thoughtful explanation; this helps them clarify their thinking. The teacher can then suggest alternatives and potential ways to proceed.

SECTION II

Using a CONCEPT to integrate art, math, science, poetry, social studies, and creative writing

PATTERN

A pattern emerges when something happens often enough to establish a certain predictability. Patterns originate from process, materials, traditions, habits, economic factors, and the attitudes and thinking of a particular period in time. Patterns may be arrangements of political events, chemical elements, words in a poem. Patterns may also be composed of abstract shapes that have a definite relationship involving some sort of repetition and consistent interval that need not always be rigid and reasonable—but rather implied and intuited.

A pattern, then, is a structure of relationships. A considerable part of the educational process both in and out of school has to do with uncovering and understanding relationships, so children should be exposed to patterning as early as kindergarten. Perceiving patterns is a way of getting beneath the surface to what is really going on. Helping children examine patterns as an integral part of living rather than as an abstract exercise is exciting because we live in patterns, are surrounded by patterns, think, move, and speak in patterns.

Patterning can be a liberation or a limitation, depending on how it is used. Consider history. The eighteenth century pattern for fighting a proper war required opposing sides to line up and march toward each other in visible formation. Within firing distance of one another, they stopped, fired reloaded, then fired again—if they were lucky enough to still be standing. In our War of Independence the British Red Coats advanced through clearings in the green wilderness in straight tight lines like a classical corps de ballet, providing perfect targets for the raggle-taggle volunteers, fighting Indian-style from behind trees and bushes. This pattern of early guerilla warfare claimed heavy British casualties and forced them to change *their* patterns of tactical warfare.

Consider Sherlock Holmes of literary fame. He could not have solved a single case without his uncanny ability to uncover relationships between disconnected and seemingly irreconcilable bits of information and evidence. He was a master pattern seeker. All good detectives are. One aspect of detective stories that fascinates us is the game-plot: we are invited to test our ability, to piece together the pattern before the detective can do so. Coincidental and far-fetched clues strengthen the suspense and challenge our powers of perception.

Anne Morrow Lindbergh observes that a good relationship between people

> has a pattern like a dance and is built on some of the same rules. The partners do not need to hold on tightly, because they move confidently in the same pattern, intricate but gay and swift and free, like a country dance of Mozart's. To touch heavily would be to arrest the pattern and freeze the movement, to check the endlessly changing beauty of its unfolding. There is no place here for the possessive clutch, the clinging arm, the heavy hand; only the barest touch in passing. Now arm in arm, now face to face, now back to back—it does not matter which. Because they know they are partners moving to the same rhythm, creating a pattern together, and being invisibly nourished by it.*

To quote another writer, Marya Mannes, "awareness of fundamental patterns of life is the measure of any real culture."

In the best sense, then, patterns are structured relationships that provide people a basis on which to proceed and within which to be inventive. Any creative process means seeking out new patterns. The following activities investigate man-made patterns and patterns shaped by material, culture, and process.

The first project, Pattern Blocks and Quilting, relates all the academic subject areas. It carries patterning through discovery and definition, an introduction to music through chanting, and into a bit of math and science. It establishes a relationship between social studies and art by examining the historical times and necessities that nurtured the American art form of quilting. This is suitable for a second- and third-grade classroom and could be developed as a unit over a two- or three-week period.

Dip and Dye is suitable for kindergarten through third grade. Pattern over Pattern can be used as a follow-up to Dip and Dye in upper first through third grade. Advanced second- and third-grade students will enjoy making a Japanese accordian book, which in turn can be used for language arts experiences, poetry, Haiku, a journal, or illustrated short stories.

---

*Anne Morrow Lindbergh, *Gift From the Sea* (Random House, Inc., 1965)

Pattern Blocks and Quilting

MATERIALS
    Two sheets of colored construction paper for each student
    Scissors
    Glue sticks or Elmer's glue
    Rulers
    Butcher paper

BOOKS
    Gutcheon, *The Perfect Patchwork Primer* (Penguin Books).
    Holstein, *The Pieced Quilt* (New York Graphics Society).
    A Teacher's Guide for PATTERN BLOCKS (ESS, Webster Division, McGraw-Hill).
    Baratta-Lorton, *Mathematics Their Way* (Addison-Wesley), Chapter 2, Pattern One, pp. 18–55; Chapter 10, Pattern Two, pp. 252–273.

FILMS
    Over and Over, Grades 1–3 (Harcourt Brace Jovanovich)

INTERRELATING
    Science using ESS Pattern Blocks in relation to patterning in American quilts
    Beginning music and poetry by patterns of chanting
    Social studies by examining how cultural patterns affect and encourage art forms

Math by working through symmetry and asymmetry as well as congruence and similarity in patterning

Language arts by using the above information as a basis for original stories

PURPOSE

Compare and manipulate shapes and colors
Explore symmetry and asymmetry
Observe importance of repeated relationship in patterning
Reproduce pattern

NEW VOCABULARY

chant
repetition
rhythm
repeat
order

PROCEDURE (2-3)

Begin pattern exploration with second- and third-grade children with this activity. Have them, using crayons, fill one-half of a sheet of newsprint (folded in half) with all kinds of lines and simple shapes (not identifiable objects) going in random directions, as if these lines and shapes didn't know what they were doing. On the second half, ask them to put these same lines and shapes into some kind of order. Don't define order for them—have them illustrate what they think is order. Compare the two drawings and ask the students what they did in the second that was different from the first. Get *them* to define order. Write their response on the board; helping a little in translation, you'll get pattern, repeat, shape, space, rhythm, and perhaps order and repetition. They will undoubtedly say they see repeats of lines, line movements, and shapes. You may have to guide them to see that the spaces between the lines often have a regularity, too. For the most part, however, they will perceive a certain rhythm in many of the second drawings because of purposeful repetition. Talk about it. Point out that they already know about order and what it means or they could not have defined it for you. We intuitively feel a sense of order and patterning, therefore we are all capable of recognizing even the most intricate patterns and relationships with practice.

If you wish to reinforce the components of pattern in the students' minds, try some chanting. Chanting is basic to both music and poetry.

Using the words on the chalkboard, divide the room into three groups.

The first group chants   PATTERN   PATTERN
simultaneously,
the second group chants SHAPE   AND   SPACE

while the third chants REPEAT REPEAT REPEAT REPEAT

Practice each part in individual groups first, then start the chanting as you would a round. After the second time through, direct one group to speak softer and another to speak louder, by raising and lowering your hands. They

use their voices just like musicians responding with their instruments to a conductor. Many variations are possible.

This chanting sets up a rhythm pattern related to all we are doing. Best of all, it can be heard and felt. Another chant might be:

REPETITION   REPETITION

RHYTHM   AND   BEAT

ORDER   ORDER   ORDER   ORDER

The words of the chants reinforce, again and again, the definition of pattern.

To make a class quilt, each child cuts a 6" × 6" square out of a piece of colored paper or wrapping paper. He measures and marks the center line between top and bottom and side and side, or folds the paper in half twice to find the two center lines. Next, he cuts on the lines as accurately as possible. Then, in two of the squares, he draws a line from opposite corners and cuts the paper in half making four triangles. There are now four triangles and two squares. At first just work with the four triangles.

With a second color of paper, he cuts another square the same size as the original and folds the center lines as before, creating a simple grid of four squares. Manipulating one triangle within each one of the squares, create as many different patterns as possible with the four triangles. There are at least sixteen combinations, perhaps more. Students may use as many or as few of the shapes as they wish. Have them explore a variety of arrangements until they are satisfied with the design.

Next, each child glues the pieces to the second square containing the grid. See if there are any duplicate designs—there should be. These completed squares are then all glued to a butcher paper backing to give the effect of a quilt. If there are enough duplicate squares, the class may choose to cluster them symmetrically among the other squares on the quilt surface.

A quilt that gives a different effect is one in which a single square is repeated. Have the class choose one square from the quilt and each student duplicate it. For the strongest impact, everyone should use the same two colors. Again assemble the squares on a backing, and compare with the first quilt.

If you have ESS Pattern Blocks, use them for the initial exploration of arrangements within a given square size. Then paper shapes can be substituted for the wooden blocks in the described procedure. The designs will be slightly different because the triangles in the ESS materials are polygons.

Just glueing the paper shapes on a square and keeping the edges straight will be a challenge for some students. Have them consider how much more difficult it would be to sew all the edges of the shapes together to make their square as pioneer women did.

Quilting History

The exploration of a traditional American art form—quilting—can relate and enhance social studies and patterning. The following short history gives a few facts about how quilting began. It may be helpful in introducing the class project, a paper quilt.

HISTORY

In the exploration of the North American continent, some historians theorize, the first French explorers, all men, sailed north to Canada for furs and adventure, and the Spanish, again all men, sailed to South America for gold and adventure. But, they say, the English and Dutch came to colonize so they brought their families.

These first settlers in America expected the climate on the east coast to be as mild as certain parts of Virginia they had heard about. The stories of the first winter hardships, the shortage of warm clothing and bed covers, is a sad story known to students of American history.

Until the 1880s, the women of a household made all bed coverings. Blankets and coverlets were not sold commercially until that time. Ship arrivals from England, as infrequent as months and years apart, forced families to make-do. Cloth was so scarce that clothing was passed from one family member to another, continually cut down for the smallest member until only scraps remained.

The colonial mother saved those precious scraps and sewed them together to make a quilt, stuffed with old rags, dry leaves, letters, or whatever she could find for insulation. When this quilt began to wear out she stuffed it into the next one—early recycling. Interestingly enough, many old quilts have been dated by the years noted on the letters used as stuffing. Because the cloth scraps were so irregular and were sewn together by shape, the quilts were called *crazy quilts* and they looked it. Later, when sheep were raised on the farms, the quilts were stuffed with fleece for warmth. In the winter, if the quilts got damp because of a leaky roof or snow coming in through an unchinked window, the kids woke up, made faces, and held their noses because the fleece was so smelly.

When the East India Company began to trade with the colonies, their ships brought calico and prints. After all the women in the family had made dresses they used the brightly colored scraps for quilting. Since there was not enough of any one print for an entire quilt, they cut the scraps into rectangles and randomly sewed them together in patterns called Bricks or Hit and Miss.

The traditional American patchwork quilt consisted of one block—say 12" × 12"—repeated continually to make an "overall" pattern. The women of the famliy sat around in the long winter evenings and worked on blocks, a convenient size for lap work. Checkerboard and Roman Stripe Zigzag were popular. The sewing of blocks began in October. They grew in number and by spring thaw there were enough for women to take to the quilting bee to be made into a quilt.

How the ladies looked forward to the quilting bees! They had spent their winter, snowbound, talking only to immediate family; with the first break in the weather, the "bees" began. Of all the social pleasures of early days like sugar boilings, corn huskings, and apple parings, the quilting bee was the favorite. Mother put on her best dress, took her blocks, a jar of her best pickled beets, six pumpkin pies, her daughters and off they went to chat and stitch and eat someone else's cooking. The young girls learned to sew quite naturally. Twelve or more quilt tops were considered absolutely necessary for a proper hope chest. In the evening, the ladies were joined by the men for a turkey spread and a dance.

The names of the quilt patterns are fascinating and the culture and concerns of the early settlers can be traced by them. A patch known as Duck Foot in the Mud in Long Island was known as Hand of Friendship in Quaker Philadelphia and as Bear's Paw in Ohio, clueing us in to regional conditions and concerns. These women's interest in the political activities of their times shows up in the titles Lincoln's Platform, Old Tippecanoe, and Star Spangled Banner. A hint of the hardships of traveling west are revealed in the several Rocky Road patterns: Rocky Road to Oklahoma, Rocky Road to Kansas, Rocky Road to California, and Texas Tears. Religious thoughts surfaced in Solomon's Temple, Joseph's Coat, and Robbing Peter to Pay Paul. For romantic names, consider Lady of the Lake, True Lover's Knot, and Lover's Links.

In colonial times quilt making was probably not thought of as "art," yet all the requirements for the evolution of a genuine folk art form were present. The quilt tradition grew out of the social, economic, and environmental needs of the times, out of the fact that American woman was skilled in sewing, that the available materials came in small swatches, and that she felt an irresistible need to create. All these conditions provided just the right mix for this practical application of pattern.

The French in Canada had furs to keep them warm; the Spanish had the South American sun. The quilt form could not have happened in either of those situations. Substantial art, inventions, and discoveries occur as responses to inner needs and outer necessities.

LANGUAGE and FOLLOW-UP ACTIVITIES

1. Make a class history quilt. In the spring, select the major class events and escapades of the past year. Have each student illustrate one in a block. This can be done with felt-tip pens on sheeting and blocks sewn together, or on paper, assembled and glued on a backing.

2. Early American quilt blocks were given original names by their designers. After each student has designed his own block, have him name it and write a short paragraph about his choice.

3. The students can do a research project on a historical, political, social, or arts person, drawing the biography on blocks instead of writing it, then assembling it in sequence.

4. A class quilt might follow the characters of a story read in class, illustrating costumes and episodes in blocks.

5. Each quilt block might be a self-portrait of a class member, which, when assembled, truly becomes a class project.

6. As a continuing project over a period of a month or two, each student might do a family-tree history of nine blocks or more. He gathers facts and data about his family by writing a relative (out of town) for information. He can also write to the state, county, and Chamber of Commerce and/or city government where he was born for some facts to translate into visuals on blocks.

This is not only good writing practice for children but receiving the information by mail is exciting and sharing the loot is a natural way to disseminate the information. To this, the student can add drawings of his present home, pets, brothers, sisters, mother, father, hobbies, and the like.

EXHIBITION FOLLOW-UP

Set up a display area and bring in some natural examples of patterning such as leaves, shells, butterflies, and birds. There are also the seasons, the moon and tide relationship, migration of animals, and so on. Contrast these with man-made patterns in posters, magazines, car detailing, van designing, topographical maps, and others. Have them look for pattern everywhere and contribute to the display.

Dip and Dye

MATERIALS:
- White tissue paper
- Styrofoam meat trays or shallow pans
- Red, blue, and yellow food coloring
- Alcohol
- Newspapers
- Salvaged cardboard (optional) cut to squares 4" × 4" or so

PURPOSE
- Clarify the concept of patterning
- Emphasize repetition and rhythm as necessary components of patterning
- Discover that individuality, chance, and method of procedure all contribute to a wide variety of patterns
- Illustrate primary into secondary color blending through the dying process
- Strengthen manual dexterity and small motor control by paper folding and cutting

BOOKS:
- Hollander, *Decorative Papers and Fabrics* (Van Nostrand Reinhold).
- Proctor, *The Principles of Pattern* (Van Nostrand Reinhold).
- Temko, *Paper—Folded, Cut, Sculpture* (Macmillan).

NEW VOCABULARY:

pattern
rhythm
shading
bright
rectangle

shapes
repetition
primary colors
square
triangle

PROCEDURE (K–3)

This technique is a blend of appealing materials and simple process that children from kindergarten through third grade find enticing. No two resulting patterns will ever be alike. The project can be made as simple or complex as you wish.

In working with young children, kindergarten and early first grade, discussing pattern after rather than before the dipping and dying has been completed has greater impact. As the papers are hung to dry, the repeated colors and shapes form patterns so dramatic and undeniable that they can be used as graphic examples.

With second- and third-grade children, some discussion before as well as after reinforces learning. Ask your class some questions: WHAT IS A PATTERN? HOW CAN YOU RECOGNIZE ONE? Someone is bound to say "lines that happen over and over" or "colors that repeat" or "stripes that have order." You can coax a number of responses, selecting definitive words and writing them on the chalkboard. Even if some replies are slightly off-target, you can turn them around or play off them in a positive way to help children discover what a pattern in.

If this approach does not bring the desired results, give the students time to look around the room for patterns in clothing, room structure, lighting fixtures, visual material, etcetera. By suggesting examples and defining why they are patterns, the students will come up with words like repetition, rhythm, repeat, recurring, and reappear.

Push the subject further. What else that we may not be able to see has a pattern? Isn't a song a pattern of sounds? What about games? Are the rules patterns for action? How about the daily school schedule—does it follow a pattern? If you have animals in the room, do they have habit patterns? Keep a running list of suggested patterns on the board to keep the subject in thought.

The dip-and-dye process begins with tissue paper. The cheapest can be used successfully; it often comes in 20″ × 28″ sheets. Cut them in half for easy handling. Have the students fold their 10″ × 14″ sheets along with you the first two times. Make a game of it by having them hold the paper up after each fold so you can tell at a glance if they have it right before proceeding.

As shown in the illustration, fold the paper in half lengthwise three times. For rectangles, fold this strip from the end in rectangular segments; fold it in squares for squares; and for triangles, fold a corner down diagonally and repeat this fold to the end of the strip.

Now for the dye. Food coloring is used because it can be washed out of clothing. It can be used full-strength but is less expensive when mixed with water or alcohol, which drys quickly. Alcohol does not saturate the paper as completely as does water and allows the delicate tissue to unfold with greater safety. Mix one part color with two parts alcohol—dilute it further for pastels. The color dries much lighter than it appears when wet. If you use the three primary colors—red, blue, and yellow—the children will discover purple, orange, and green as they dip in the basic colors, which partially blend. As illustrated, the folded shapes are dipped to corners and edges. Then, they are placed between two pieces of cardboard or several layers of newspaper and stepped on to press out excess water or alcohol. This technique can still be successful if the folded shapes are set aside to dry, omitting the cardboard step. However, the designs will not be as intricate or precise.

HELPFUL SUGGESTIONS

Reduce spilling by pouring the color mixture into Styrofoam meat trays, or any kind of shallow pan, and keeping the mixture 1/8" deep. Set up a dye table covered with newspapers to catch drips.

Suggest the children hold the rectangle in the center and watch the color creep up toward their fingers. Tell them to take it out before it touches the fingers. This is important. Otherwise, they will immerse and saturate the paper and the pattern color becomes muddy.

The children's next temptation is to open the wet folded paper immediately, which will tear into colored shreds. Have each student cover his desk with newspaper; make a rule that all wet papers must be laid on the newspaper for 30 to 45 minutes. If they are still slightly damp when you finally open them, hang them on a wire or clothes line stretched across the room. The endlessly varied patterns and colors will dramatically emphasize repetition and rhythm.

Pattern on Pattern

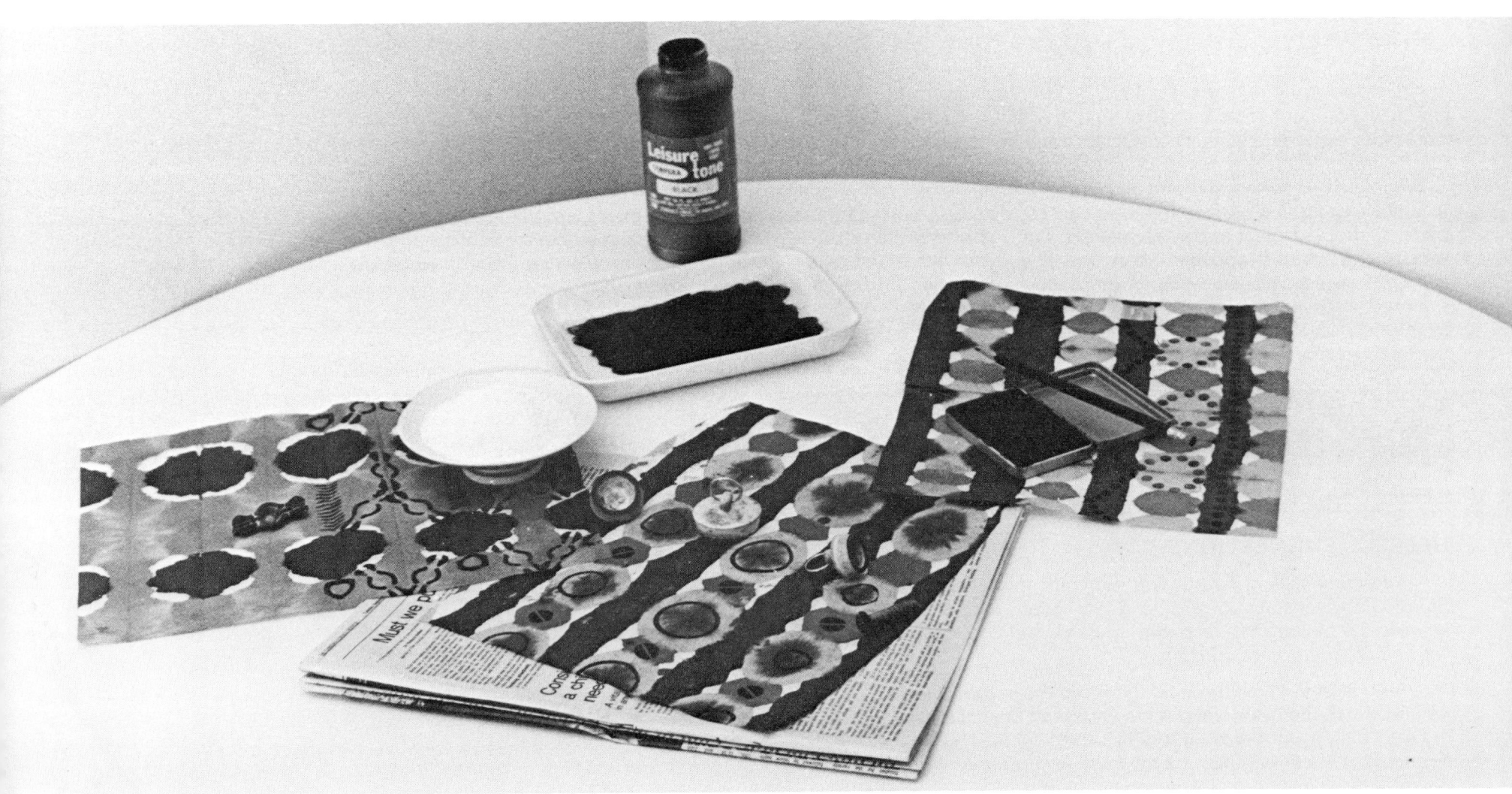

An extension of the Dip and Dye activity

MATERIALS
Same as for Dip and Dye
Gadgets for printing
Tempera paint
Detergent
Foam rubber, not over ½" thick

PURPOSE
Correlating dying and printing techniques
Arranging and sequencing color
Developing one pattern out of another

NEW VOCABULARY
overprint
grid
alternate
sequence

PROCEDURE (2-3)

This activity explores pattern on pattern. It is a valuable extension of the previous experience for second- and third-graders. The folding, dipping, and dying is repeated a second time. They now know the process and are ready to experiment with folding, and with color and its placement. Too often students have only one opportunity to try a technique; and by the time they generate a couple of ideas it's time to clean up. This serves as a welcome second chance. The intention is to print over the pattern already created by the folding and dying. Children are usually reluctant to print over the first dip-dye pattern sheets because they are totally satisfying as they stand. In a second session, when they are ready to try something new, the sheet can be a grid on which to stamp further patterns with gadgets, erasers, innertube shapes, or potatoes.

To start the printing, place the dyed paper on several thicknesses of newspaper for best results (the newspapers act as a cushion). Make a stamp pad by cutting a piece of foam rubber, not over ½" thick, to fit a Styrofoam meat tray. Pour tempera over the foam rubber and work it in. When any gadget is pressed into the surface it will yield just enough color to print without dripping. If the tempera is too thin and seeps to the bottom of the pad, mix in a little detergent to give it body and it will hold on the surface.

Various sizes of sink stoppers and other simple shapes, even lead pencil erasers, are fine gadgets to use. Existing color patterns can suggest places to print: in the center of color repeats on the grid, between them, or across both. The children can place stamps in alternating squares and alternate or sequence sizes of stoppers. They can stamp the pencil eraser, which makes polka dots, to ring existing shapes or run along the creases. There are endless possibilities; the students will find them.

Japanese Accordion Book

MATERIALS
    Scrap cardboard
    Butcher paper strips, 5" × 30"
    Two sheets of dip and dyed paper for each student
    Elmer's glue (diluted)
    1" wide brushes

BOOKS
    Ogawa, *Forms of Paper* (Reinhold).
    Haiku for children: Behn, trans., *Cricket Songs;* and *More Cricket Songs* (Harcourt Brace Jovanovich).

INTERRELATING
    Language arts—the form of the book encourages a fresh approach to story writing.

PURPOSE
    Experiment with thoughts and illustrations within a new format
    Explore the construction of a book form used in another culture

NEW VOCABULARY
    Haiku

PROCEDURE (2-3)

Making a Japanese accordion book out of two sheets of this dyed paper seems quite fitting because the pattern and texture look oriental.

Scrap cardboard makes the hardback covers and one continuous strip of butcher paper, folded accordion-style, constitutes the pages. Keeping it size small holds the materials to a minimum and makes it easier for the students to handle. For a 5" × 5" book, cut two pieces of cardboard to this square size. Glue one square on top of the first 5" and one on the last 5" of the paper strip. Keeping the measurement square avoids placement problems. A 20" strip remains. When the glue is almost dry, fold the paper accordion-style using the cardboard as the unit of measure. Then glue the dyed tissue to the reverse side of the cardboard square. Leave the book unfolded while drying to prevent it from sticking together in the wrong places.

For ease in the glueing process, set out a diluted mixture of two parts Elmer's glue to one part water and several 1" wide brushes. When glueing either the butcher paper or the tissue, paint the entire surface of the 5" × 5" cardboard with glue, then place the paper on top and paint over that surface as well. With tissue, work fast for the color runs. A bit of bleeding is attractive—too much is a disaster. Since the brushes tend to pick up this color, rinse between glueing each booklet.

The pages may be used as individual units for writing, however, the book's form lends itself to one long continuous story with illustrations running across all four pages. Flip it over to write a second story on the reverse side then fold it again and put a title on both covers.

This is an appropriate time to introduce the students to haiku. Have them copy several of the short, fragile, thoughtful poems into their book. The poems thus transcribed become their own. This introduction prepares the way for future writing of haiku when the students are mature enough to understand more about its subtle form.

CAMOUFLAGE

Camouflage is the act of disguise, of having something appear as something else for the purpose of concealment. It's hiding in plain sight. We generally think of it as being used during war. Commandos attacking by night smear their clothes and faces with mud to become less visible; on naval duty, ships are painted a light and dark gray pattern to blend in with the sky and the sea. But many other kinds of camouflage exist, for instance, a wolf in sheep's clothing, or covering embarrassment with laughter. A chameleon changes color and mood to blend in with his environment. So do some people. A more concrete example is a white polar bear, as hard to spot on an ice floe as a zebra is in the striped African bush. Translating vital messages into codes and ciphers to elude the enemy, and wearing masks to transform ourselves and fool our public is all part of the great cover-up.

Stepping into the camouflage experience with children is easily done with masks. These have given Halloween its aura of mystery and otherworldliness that kids find fascinating. The first activity takes advantage of this Halloween experience by using masks as a vehicle for developing creative thought processing. Animal and Insect Camouflage sets up the problem of providing a safe environment for either and requires working through problems of color, pattern, shape, and size relationships. The third activity, Camouflage a Painting, creates a focal point for inducing verbalization and a free exchange of ideas while sharpening observation skills. The formulation of each of these is loose enough to fit kindergarten through third grade with only minor adjustments. However, the fourth activity, Secret Message Camouflage, is best presented at second- or third-grade level and up, because the students must be able to read and spell reasonably well. It will also improve their abilities in these areas.

For Animals and Insects

MATERIALS
Colored construction paper
Old science books or nature magazine (for pictures)
Three dimensional scrap material—twigs, toothpicks, feathers, etc.
Glue
Small boxes (optional)

BOOKS
Farb and Peter et al., *The Insects* (Time-Life Inc.).
Poling, *Animals in Disguise* (Norton).
Swain, *Insects in Their World* (Doubleday).
Tison and Taylor, *Animal Hide-and-Seek* (World Publishing).

INTERRELATING
Science—insect characteristics and habits pertaining to camouflage as a protective device

PURPOSE
Practice in distinguishing between similarities and differences in pattern, color, and dark-light contrasts
Apply facts learned in one subject area (science) to a related activity in another (art)

NEW VOCABULARY
camouflage	contrast
chameleon	similar
disguise	different
blend	

PROCEDURE (K–3)

Camouflage in the natural world of animals and insects is a protective device, taking many forms. The use of color to confuse and conceal is common. Some animals change color to match their surroundings. The chameleon, a quick-change artist, responds immediately to his background; the frogs, lizards, fish, and spiders having this ability take more time for the transformation. The yellow crab spider hides in the swamp buttercup. When he moves to a white flower he changes to a white color but it takes five or six days. Some grasshoppers and stick-shaped insects change color over the span of their lives, beginning as green in the spring and summer for protection and turning brown in the fall. In spring and summer they eat leaves containing chlorophyll and in the fall they live on brown leaves, so their diet may have something to do with the cycle.

Another protective device are markings that disguise shape. If the animal's markings emphasize its shape, it tends to stand out from the background. However, if the markings run off its edges into the background it is difficult for the hunter's eye to differentiate the shape. Zebras and butterflies are examples. Their markings allow them to fade into the background so successfully their exact position is hard to distinguish. Snakes are striped and spotted for the same reason. Although successful at blending into the surrounding visual patterns, these mammals, insects, and reptiles must conceal their shadows, which will give them away. Some turn profile into the sun to cast the thinnest possible shadow.

Yet another way of concealing identity is to imitate another species. Wasps have stingers and several varieties of beetles taste so bad that predators avoid both. Some insects adopt the "look" of these wasps or beetles in the hope of survival. Then, there is the caterpiller that looks like a twig, the katydid that looks like a leaf, and the frog that looks like bark.

Use the idea of camouflage as basis for a thoughtful activity. Find some old science books or nature magazines and give each student a page with the picture of a mammal, insect, or reptile to cut out. He is to provide the safest possible color and texture environment for his charge. For a two-dimensional collage, have the students start by placing their cut-outs on a compatible color of construction paper (their choice of course).

With a little research, the student can create a representational environment, taking into consideration the kind of habitat the animal requires. On the other hand, he might choose an imaginary environment, perhaps including other fantasy animals. One important rule: at least half the animal must be exposed. Its surroundings may include colored shapes, and textures cut from construction paper, magazine illustrations, or they can be actual three-dimensional materials—twigs, toothpicks, feathers, and all that other good stuff that has accumulated (just so it can be glued to paper).

If your class has already made two-dimensional collages, perhaps they would prefer working in three dimensions. Collect some boxes to provide every student with a top or bottom in which to make a small shadow box diorama. Again, real or imagined textures and shapes can be used. Remind the students that the safety of their animal depends on their ability to camouflage and disguise his presence.

This activity leads to discoveries about related colors, about low and high contrast, about size and pattern visibility. If the animal or insect is small, he is less readily seen in company with other small objects. Similarity is safe. Standing out in a crowd or the jungle may be admired, but it's always chancy.

Have a display of the finished habitats. Which comes closest to looking like a real world? Which is the most fantastic? Discuss some of the devices used to conceal the animals.

Spin off some creative writing from the activity. The class might write a paragraph about one of the "worlds" or each student might write about his favorite. Get things moving with some questions: WHERE IS THIS PLACE? FROM WHAT OR WHOM IS THE ANIMAL HIDING? WHAT IS HE THINKING? DOES HE BELIEVE YOU CAN SEE HIM? Read these to the class or place each by the appropriate diorama so the students may read them.

For Kids·Masks

MATERIALS
- Butcher paper
- Stapler
- Masking tape
- String
- Elmer's glue
- Paint
- Crayons
- Felt-tip pens
- Scissors
- All kinds of scrap materials
- Colored construction paper

BOOKS
- Bihalji-Merin, *Great Masks* (Abrams, Inc.).
- Lommel, *Masks: Their Meaning and Function* (McGraw-Hill).
- Baranski, *Masks* (Davis Press).
- Grater, *Paper Faces* (Taplinger).
- Alkema, *Masks* (Sterling Pub.).
- Liberté, *Masks* (Van Nostrand Reinhold).

INTERRELATING
Social studies—history and the use of masks in cultures around the world.

PURPOSE
- Generate, organize, and facilitate ideas in group situation
- Listen for and process new points of view
- Analyze and evaluate suggestions and opinions
- Strengthen decision-making ability

NEW VOCABULARY
- Kabuki
- Ño
- Mardi Gras
- carnival
- character (as in a play)
- Commedia dell'Arte

PROCEDURE (K–3)

Masks have a long history. Fragments of animal masks can be seen in European cave paintings of the Old Stone Age. Speculation suggests these were either used by hunters to gain silent entrance to a mystic animal world in tribal rites or by dancers to gain the animal's attributes: strong as a bull or fierce as a tiger. Primitives were attracted to the use of masks. So are kids because a mask can have a liberating effect, freeing one to speak and act and think in new ways.

Substantial segments of social studies can be taught through the study of masks, beginning with the False Face Society of the Iroquois, the Mandan, North West Coast Indians, Mayans, and Aztecs, who used masks for everything from casting magic spells to healing. Medicine men wore masks to frighten away diseases. Jump continents to Africa and examine the masks that influenced much modern art, beginning with Picasso. Each had its identifiable style based on culture, religion, and purpose. The Greeks used masks for dramatic effect. They staged plays in huge amphitheaters; many spectators seated in the back could not see the subtle changes on the actors' faces, but they could see masks and read the expressions. There were no women actors at that time so men (masq)ueraded as females. Other countries with a tradition of using masks in drama and mime are Tibet, Japan, with Kabuki and Ño Theater, and the Italians of the Commedia dell'Arte.

Carnival and Mardi Gras mean masking for fun; knight's helmets, space suits, and gas masks mean war. Labor provides welder's, diver's, astronaut's, and sur-

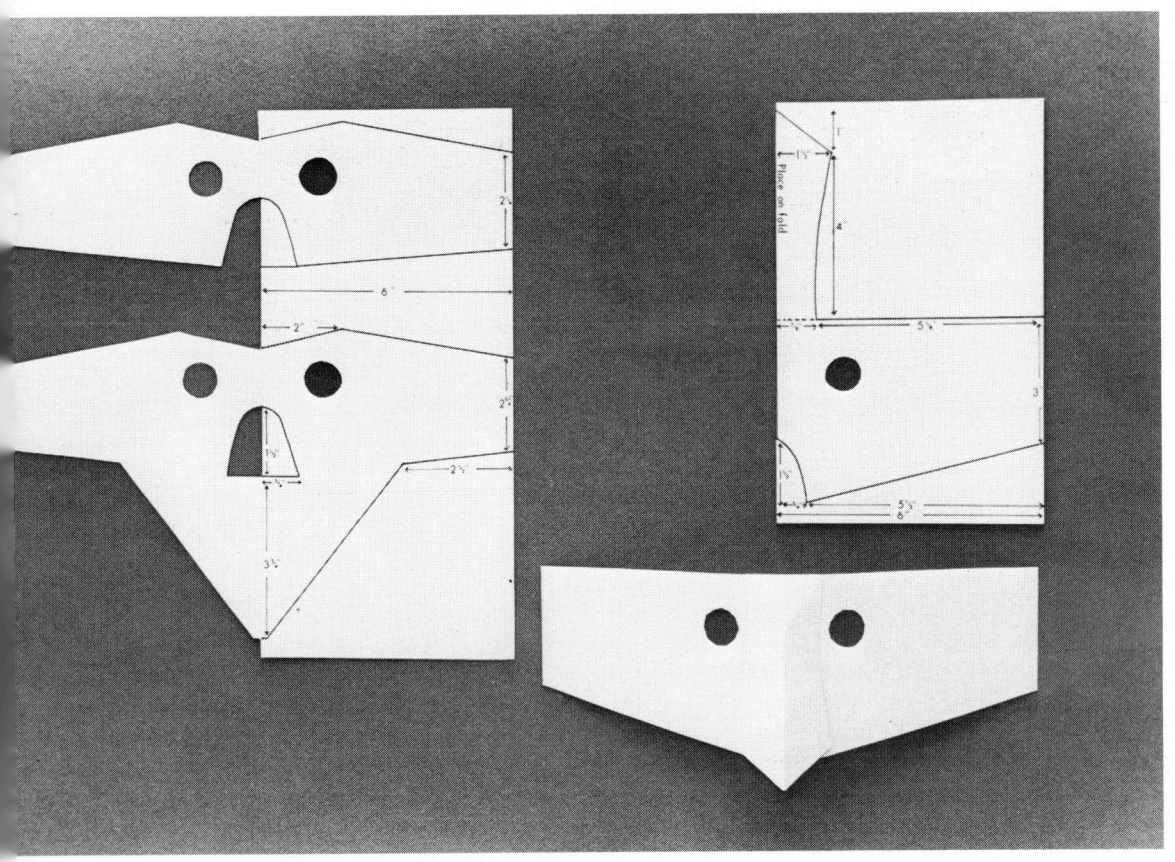

geon's masks, and in sports we find the baseball catcher's, the skier's, and the motorcyclist's goggle masks. Oh yes—for a beauty mask there's the mud pack.

How many of these do your students know about? Start a discussion by drawing out all the information they have about masks, including history, purpose, appearance, and materials. Enlarge upon it. Photographs, drawings, and books illustrating how people use masks can excite their imaginations. Let them be thinking about these things as they help you set up a materials table with butcher paper, paint, crayons, felt-tip pens, scissors, and all the paraphernalia you have been collecting that can be glued, pasted, taped, or tied to a base.

Divide the students into groups by color or number coding. In this way, new groups will be formed, splitting up twosomes who usually work together, and provide greater opportunity for children's fresh ideas to emerge. A free flow of ideas and materials is necessary for shifting into new patterns of thinking but the stage must be set carefully or the excitement may spill into chaos.

Before the students get their group instructions, give the class some general information. Make it clear that each person is to make his own mask, covering the whole head or only part of it. The illustrated patterns may be used as bases on which to work (have such patterns available for tracing and use tagboard or something heavier than construction paper for this). However, since the process of conceptualization and invention is important, welcome innovations. There should be no restrictions as long as the mask meets the requirement of wearability and relationship to the group theme.

Another suggestion is to cut old sheeting into large circles, which can be decorated and eye-holed, then pulled over the head, gathered and tied around the neck with yarn or string. Ask a volunteer to be tied up in a circle-sheet so the others can see how it looks when worn. This makes designing easier. The appearance is just odd enough to jostle the imagination. Spark the group by asking what the mask reminds them of. They may say onion tops, insect heads, or space things, among others. Push for many suggestions. SHOULD THE FACE BE ON THE TOP OR THE SIDE? SHOULD THERE BY MORE THAN ONE? For the actual decorating, felt-tip pens and crayons are easy to use on sheeting.

OTHER APPROACHES

Since a provocative assignment is a basic element of a successful activity, give each group its own set of instructions, which it must figure out and execute. Here are some examples:

Group 1 works around a table with a selection of hats. These may be contributions of students and faculty, or prize selections from Volunteers of America or the Salvation Army. Have each student select an irresistible hat, get acquainted with it, and ask himself who might wear it. Encourage the students to exchange ideas, even weird ones. These may form a path to fantasy, the animal world, a character in life or on television. Each student

then builds his mask to accommodate the hat. When the masks are finished, the group (all the groups) will present themselves to the class in mime: they might be passengers on a bus going home after work. They can line up chairs and set the scene just as they want it. Knowing they are to share their creation with the class, they will exercise some sense of overall design to conclude the activity.

Group 2 will work from a record having a number of characters. For example, a dance record that includes several animals is "The Lobster Quadrille" from Columbia Children's Library, recorded by Carly and Lucy Simon. It introduces a crab, whiting, snail, porpoise, lobster, and turtle. A simple way for these students to make their masked presentation to the class is to dance a chorus, each moving in rhythm in ways representative of his animal. The selection of these characteristic movements will take some directed discussion and rehearsal. It also calls for some original thinking. Incidentally, if an animal or character in any group requires more than a mask for identification (a good crab must also have two claws), encourage the students to go beyond masking. Construction paper and masking tape or a stapler make almost any shape possible.

Group 3 will use a favorite poem or short story as a basis for this group creation; one child will read it in part or full, while the rest mime for the benefit of the total class. Near Halloween, James Whitcomb Riley's *The Gobble-uns'll git you ef you don't watch out!* (Lippincott) makes a usable story. The cast of characters includes "Little Orphant Annie" who narrates, and some assorted goblins. Since the goal is to get the students to pool thoughts and plan strategies of their own, have the group go over the story chosen, looking for action to translate movement and mime. Have them experiment with some ideas. Henri Matisse once advised, "Don't wait for inspiration. It comes while one is working."

The teacher must decide the number of groups that will work at one time. Children benefit by playing the role of both participant and spectator, seeing and hearing what other students think and do. Some classrooms can accommodate several groups while the teacher and/or aides float and assist. Others will require a teacher or aide in constant attendance—in kindergarten perhaps only two groups are needed. Whatever the decision, do take advantage of the group performance-presentation, because it gives working together real purpose.

For Teachers - Masks

MATERIALS
   Paper plates
   Felt-tip pen

PURPOSE
   A teaching device for the teacher

PROCEDURE

A child or an adult puts a mask on and soon inhibitions begin to slip away and shyness or quietness fades. Observation reveals that people say things in this context that they could rarely say in any other—honest and telling things. Strangely enough, the listener invariably responds with tolerance. Perhaps it's because the mask impersonalizes the comments. They can have validity without malice. Whatever the psychological reason, why not use masks as a teaching aid?

Suppose you want to present a new concept in math so the class will remember it well, or you want to do a mock reaction in a discussion about behavior. Masks can be used to intensify and clarify the experience. To make them, draw simple faces on the bottom of four paper plates with a broad felt-tip pen. The faces represent anger, sadness, pleasure, and surprise, as shown in the illustration. NOTE: The photograph shows examples of masks that indicate emotions. You will want to create masks in your own style. On the top of the plate, write "anger," etcetera, to coincide with the face in top-up position. This makes it easy for you to choose the correct plate, in position, to hold in front of your face.

If you are discussing values or social behavior with the class, during the question and answer period, try varying your verbal responses with a mask response (even if the dialogue is only among the students). The mask response, by its very nature, will be exaggerated, which heightens the effect and makes a strong impression, aiding the students in retention of important points. It is totally visual, candid, and for the most part, impersonal. For the student, there are no words to play off, no shades of meaning or interpretation, none of the usual mannerisms or facial expressions that subtly reveal the teacher's feelings. The student must resort to his own thoughts and opinions. Addressing these to a paper-plate-face is less than fulfilling, so the students are forced to talk and listen to each other. You can moderate the discussion from the outside until you wish to participate or summarize. In this way, many of the students' suppressed and troubling questions can be aired—good humor will generally prevail.

You can also use the mask idea to reinforce concepts in math, science, or any subject area. It is a good way to review material with questions, answers, and a light touch. In this case, use the masks consistently to convey an immediate reaction and follow up with as much or little verbal information you think is needed. The less verbal the response, the more readily will the students volunteer their knowledge. You can get an idea of how much they know and how well they know it.

This masking is a bit of a game, but a purposeful one. It shouldn't be used too often because the novelty and surprise are important to success.

For Works of Art

MATERIALS
    A reproduction of a painting
    Two pieces of cardboard, the same size or larger
    Tape
    Scissors

INTERRELATING
    Social studies, speaking, and language arts

PURPOSE
    Refine observation skills
    Stretch the imagination
    Develop inductive reasoning processes
    Theorize and speculate about evidence
    Practice in expressing points of view
    Sharing feelings

NEW VOCABULARY
    fantasy
    reality

PROCEDURE (K–3)

    Looking at good reproductions of paintings, both old masters and contemporary works, is an excellent way to learn about the visual arts, history, and the world. They can also stir up some amazing conjectures and exchanges among the students, giving them much-needed practice in expressing their feelings and points of view.

    It is usually easy for children to understand twentieth century art. Because an artist like Paul Klee paints

with humor and the appearance of innocence, children respond to his paintings immediately. Reproductions of his work are fairly easy to find. Another modern example is the work of Friedensreich Hundertwasser, which projects an aura of fantasy with pure color and active line in which students find much to discuss. Then too, some of the current children's books have marvelous illustrations.

We're going to camouflage the reproduction or illustration, then reveal it bit by bit to the class with a little suspense and a lot of conversation. Of course the larger the repro the better. To prepare it for class, back it with cardboard and place another thin piece of cardboard or tagboard over the top. A black top covering is most effective, but a lighter color is acceptable. Decide where the four or six most provocative areas of the reproduction are and cut a rectangular or square window out of the top cardboard directly over these areas. Try to include just enough information about color, line, space, and texture to tickle the imagination without revealing the entire idea or object. You can do exactly the same thing with reproductions from past centuries if you wish to integrate painting with history and culture (it's almost impossible to separate them). Choose areas with parts of costumes, old-fashioned shoes, and hats, or objects of the period like parts of old carriages, boats, and palaces.

Next, place the cut-out piece back over the window and tape it across the top or sides. It may be easier to tape a 3" × 5" card or a piece of construction paper (same color) over the opening. To use this peep show, lift one card at a time so the class can see through the window. You will be amazed by the speculation and conversation, the implications and theories that result from childrens' efforts to identify what is going on, where, and when. These may involve time, space, style of painting, and coloration, which may tell something about mood or weather. There really is no limit to the inferences, and all the while observation skills are being refined. You may need to give an occasional clue to expand directions or focus thought, depending on your teaching goals for the activity. It's like solving a mystery with several clues at a time. The information from the second window may alter or support the conjecture stimulated by the first. One interpretation will trigger another; when the children realize all comments will be given equal consideration they become increasingly thoughtful and let their imaginations race. Write some of this information on the board as you go for easy recall and reference. It has been said that a fine painting is a source of experience. The depth of thought, feeling, and execution of a master work will provide visual material for a wide range of responses.

If you wish to introduce a new book to spark interest and prepare the way for careful listening, use an illustration from the book in this way.

For Secret Messages

MATERIALS
Paper and pencil

BOOKS
Sarnoff and Ruffins, *The Code and Cipher Book* (Scribner's).
Rothman and Tremain, *Secrets with Ciphers and Codes* (Macmillan).
Lamb, *Secret Writing Tricks* (Thomas Nelson).
Peterson, *How to Write Codes and Send Secret Messages* (Four Winds).
Kohn, *Secret Codes and Ciphers* (Prentice-Hall).

INTERRELATING
Math—patterning and working with decoding and substitution of numbers for letters
Social studies—historical references to the uses of codes and ciphers

PURPOSE
Develop pattern recognition
Sharpen reading and observation skills

NEW VOCABULARY

code	symbol
cipher	decode
patterns	encipher
Julius Caesar	decipher
cryptography	

PROCEDURE (2–3)

Cryptography is the science of secret communication. A message, to be secret, must be disguised or camouflaged in some way. There are two basic camouflaging methods—ciphers and codes. Their use has literally changed the course of history: they have caused and averted wars, they have won and lost battles. Because they are still very much in use today, every government, including the British (Scotland Yard) and the U.S. (FBI), employs a group of cryptologists.

In a cipher the usual order of letters is systematically rearranged by substituting characters, symbols, or other letters for the correct alphabet letters. To convert a written text into a cipher text is called *enciphering*. *Deciphering* reverses the procedure and converts a cipher text into a written text. In a cipher, every letter of the original message is replaced.

A secret code is slightly different in that it is a method of communication other than a cipher by which one person transmits information to another. A group of letters can be substituted for syllables, words, phrases, or sentences. In this case, a code book is necessary. Or, coding may appear as a system of signals for communication by telegraph or semaphore.

Whatever the method is, it is secret and mysterious and that's the attraction. It suggests spies and intrigue—most of us find that irresistible. Many stranger-than-fiction stories are told about breaking wartime codes. The Japanese code was broken by U.S. Intelligence officers in World War II, who spent months patiently examining and manipulating the code for clues to the key. They kept quiet about the discovery while Japanese command orders to their fleet maneuvering in the South Pacific were monitored and countered by our fleet, contributing to the eventual defeat of the Japanese.

To decipher or break a code, one looks for patterns. Students coding and decoding practice develops pattern recognition. It sharpens their reading and observation skills and develops patience. In the recent past, people studied and invented codes and ciphers as a hobby for all these reasons plus the fact that they found it relaxing but challenging, just as crossword puzzles and acrostics are challenging.

Choose a code or cipher for the week. Write it on the board for reference then give assignments and answers to occasional problems in cipher text. This will enliven any activity. After the students have learned and worked with two or three, let them figure out which one is being used by looking for patterns.

Let's examine three simple ciphers. The first is a transposition cipher: it merely changes the normal position of the units or letters. Most kids have tried spelling their names backwards, a simple transposition cipher. Another easy one is the Chinese cipher. It derives its name from the fact that the message runs up and down columns, like Chinese writing. Suppose our message is: The class will have story time after recess. There are 36 letters. Arbitrarily divide them into six columns of six letters each (they could as easily be divided into three columns of twelve, four columns of nine, etcetera). Begin on the right and write down six letters. Move to the left and start a column of six letters, writing up. Continuing in this way, it would look like this:

```
s e m h l t
s a i a l h
e f t v i e
c t y e w c
e e r s s l
r r o t s a
```

The cipher written out would look like this:
Semhlt saialh eftvie ctyewc eerssl rrotsa.

The early Greeks created a secret cipher by squaring the alphabet into five rows of five letters each. This left out one letter so they made *I* and *J* the same since *J* was rarely used. They numbered each horizontal and vertical row from one to five. It looked like this:

```
  1 2 3 4 5
1 A F L Q V
2 B G M R W
3 C H N S X
4 D I O T Y
5 E K P U Z
```

To encipher a message, they found the letter needed by the numbers of intersecting rows. The number on the left, from the vertical row of numbers, was always given first; therefore, *H* would be 32 and *Q* would be 14. Decode this message:

45 43 54   41 51 31 42 53 32 51 24 51 41   44 32 51   23 51 34 34 11 22 51.

The numbers were usually redistributed into groups of five, making the code even more inscrutable:

45435 44151 31425 33251 24514 14432 51235 13434 11225 1.

A third cipher was invented by Julius Caesar and is called a *substitution cipher*. He moved each letter of the original message down the alphabet three places, thus *A* becomes *D* and *F* becomes *I*. If you want to write READ in this cipher, it looks like UHDG.

SECTION III
Using a MATERIAL to integrate art, social studies, math, and science

PAPER

You can cut, curl, and crumple it
paint, print, and pleat,
You can flute, fasten, and fold it
with a twist and tear technique.

You can stretch, score, and shape it
wad, wave, and weave,
The possibilities of paper
are hard to believe.

And, it all began in China about A.D. 105 when Ts'ai Lun, the court's chief eunuch, tired of carving history on wooden tablets, gathered the bark of a mulberry bush, a few old rags, and fish nets, crushed them in a mortar to separate the fibers, mixed in some water, and stirred. This paper batter was ladled into forms on cloth bats, like making square pancakes on a griddle. Then the thin papercakes were peeled off the cloth, dried between felts, and called sheets of paper. The Chinese initiated the use of paper for state records, correspondence, and money. Recent digs in China have revealed suits of armor from around this period made of papier-mâché so hard it could resist arrows and sword blades.

In the eighth century, the Moslems sweeping across the East like a whirlwind out of the desert picked up paper-making in China and the zero in India and carried them both back to Spain. The process had come to Europe. A mill set up in Fabriano, Italy in 1276 still makes handsome paper bearing its watermark today.

Early paper-making procedure depended on the skills of three men. The vatman stirred the vat of pulp, dipped in the mold, then shook it to distribute the pulp evenly and release the excess water. The coucher removed the sheet from the mold, and couched or laid the wet paper on a piece of felt in one flat, unwrinkled sheet. The layman peeled it from the felt and placed it in a neat pile, which was then transferred to a press that squeezed out remaining water. Drying was the final step.

Today, close to 7,000 different kinds of paper are sold commercially. It is a material so versatile as to challenge imagination and skills at every level of development. Because it is such a common, available material it is often overlooked as a potential for innovation and experimentation.

Making paper is a logical place to start our exploration. First graders can do a simple version that makes it their very own process. The next activity involves innertube prints, alphabet stamps, and collage on brown paper bags. This is followed by an activity making chop marks, similar to trademarks, which are made into printing stamps for individual identification.

As soon as children can manipulate scissors, imaginative paper cutting and folding provides the opportunity for refining scissors skill and coordinating mind and hand. Wax-Dipped Forms are most appealing and make a fine holiday activity since they simulate a stained glass window. Equation Necklaces combine math and craft suitable for third grade: making the beads without the math component is possible for second grade. Second- and third-graders can handle Ozalid Blueprints and Papier-Mâché Fruit and Vegetables very well.

Making Paper

MATERIALS
    Newspaper
    Dishpan
    Mixing bowl
    Egg beater
    Tablespoon measure
    Cornstarch or wallpaper paste
    4" × 4" piece of screenwire (one for each child if possible)
    Clover leaves and blades of tall grass (optional)

INTERRELATING
    Social studies—history of invention and development of paper

PURPOSE
    Learn a sequential process
    Recognize how recycling works

NEW VOCABULARY
    vatman
    coucher (pronounced coocher)
    layman

PROCEDURE (1–3)

Making paper in the classroom moves very smoothly if a little preliminary work is begun a week before. Bring a dishpan to class and fill it with six cups of water. Have the students tear three single sheets of newsprint into ½" pieces and drop them in water. Swish them around until they're covered with liquid and let this stand for three or four days to help break down the fibers. You can use it sooner, but it is easier to work with after standing. Have several students take turns beating the wet paper with an egg beater (an electric blender is preferable if you have one). This transforms it into a thin pulp or "slurry." Dissolve four tablespoons of cornstarch or wallpaper paste in a cup of water, pour it back into the pulp, and stir. This can sit a couple of days or until you are ready to use it. The slurry is then diluted with 12 more cups of water and may be divided in half for easier access. Each child needs a 4" × 4" square of screenwire (nonaluminum is preferable because it is stiffer, but aluminum will work), which is held horizontally then dipped into the slurry—the containers must be large enough to accommodate these. Now stir the mixture by hand until cloudy with pulp. Lower the screenwire into this mixture then raise it. A layer of 1/8" to 1/10" should be distributed evenly across the screen. If it is too thick, add a little water and redip. Then place the screen on newspapers on the floor. Place a piece of oiled paper or plastic wrap, larger than the screen, on top of it and carefully roll it with a rolling pin or press with a block of wood or hands. This forces the water into the newspapers. Allow the "paper" to dry, then peel off the plastic and the screenwire.

An exciting possibility for a second sheet is to imbed small tender new leaves, like clover leaves, and blades of tall grass in the sheet. These should be placed on the slurry just before it is covered with the oiled paper and pressed. The pressing step forces the leaves into the mixture and they dry there. If a leaf drops off after the paper is dry, just tip it back into its grooves with a spot of Elmer's glue.

Keep any slurry left from the first batch and try some experiments. Have the students bring in some lint from a clothes dryer and thoroughly mix it into the pulp with an egg beater. The mixture can also be colored with food coloring either in the dishpan or by sprinkling drops of color on the slurry before it is covered with the paper and pressed.

These directions will serve a class of 25 to 30. If you do not wish to make that much, a basic recipe consists of two cups of water, one single sheet of newsprint, one tablespoon of cornstarch—then beat or blend and add four or five cups of water.

Brown Paper Bags and Innertubes

MATERIAL
- Brown paper lunch bags
- Colored construction paper
- Yarn or ribbon
- Two or more ink brayers
- Waterproof block printing ink
- Aluminum foil or tagboard
- A bicycle or automobile tire innertube
- Cardboard or recycled wood blocks
- Scissors

INTERRELATING
- Language arts through poetry printing and vowel identification

PURPOSE
- Learn a sequential process for reproducing an image
- Compose and arrange rubber stamp shapes for effect
- Understand how printing is done and the idea of reversal with letters
- Explore printing and collage on a three-dimensional surface

NEW VOCABULARY
- printing plate
- reversal
- brayer

PROCEDURE (1-3)

Paper and printing seem to go hand in hand. This activity, innertube printing on the ever-available brown paper lunch bag, combines both. This bag makes a fine, functional, three-dimensional surface for printing and the brown background is enough of a color shift from white or bright colors to produce new effects. Gadget printing works well on bags and appeals to kindergarten and first-grade students. It is described at length in the section on Pattern. It produces a less precise print than innertube, which provides clear images with precise edges. First, a suggestion: do invest in one or two inexpensive brayers or ink rollers. Children find this tool and printing ink (water base in a tube) captivating. A short examination of the process can create such anticipation that the students will tend to be more thoughtful about their design and careful in printing it. The graphic process carries with it a mysticism. Reproducing one image after another is a kind of magic.

Pick up some throw-away innertubes from a bike shop or a gas station and cut into 2" × 4" or 3" × 5" pieces, one per child. From these they may cut pumpkins, leaves, birds, letters, or whatever they can draw in simple outline. The bike innertube is particularly easy to cut with a scissors because it is so thin. With Elmer's glue, attach the pieces to cardboard *slightly* larger than the shape for ease of handling, thus creating a kind of rubber stamp. Be sure the glue is dry before printing, or the innertube will float off the base. Actually, a small 2" × 2" block of wood is perfect if you can find some scrap lumber because the sides provide a surface to grip. The students can use one 2" × 2" surface for shapes as well as both ends of the block, giving them three different surfaces to print. The cardboard or wooden base is called the *printing plate*. If cardboard and innertube are plentiful let them make several cutouts. When printing, they can arrange these in a variety of ways and trade prints with their friends.

For the inking pad, use a hard surface paper like tagboard or wrap a large book or two (as many as you have brayers) in two layers of aluminum foil. Squeeze about one inch of printing ink on surfaces and distribute it by rolling the brayer through the ink. Lift the brayer between each roll for even spreading. Caution the students to roll the ink over as small an area as practical; otherwise, it will dry too quickly and be wasted. When the brayer is fully charged (totally inked), lay the plate with the innertube cutout face up on a piece of newspaper. Roll the brayer over the face once or twice until no black rubber shows. Place the brown bag on a stack of three or four sections of newspaper on the floor, lay the printing plate face down on the bag, and step on it. Easy does it—be sure the plate does not move under your foot.

For best results, have two colors of ink at separate locations in the room, making it physically difficult to mix the colors. Make a rule that students use only one color on one stamp. Some will ask if they can combine colors. Experimentation is best done toward the end of printing. After every student has had two good color runs, let them fill half the roller with one color and half with the second to try overprinting, or whatever else they can think of.

The beauty of using water-base ink is this: when finished printing, the students can clean the brayers by holding them under the water faucet; the aluminum foil can be unwrapped from the books and thrown away, as can the tagboard.

An extension of this activity is to make letter stamps. Each student gets a piece of cardboard exactly the same size, say 1½" × 1", and is assigned one letter of the alphabet, or two if the class is small. Students cut the letters, all capital or all lower-case, from innertube to fit the cardboard. Several other students cut punctuation marks. They then glue all letters and marks on the small cardboard pieces. When the letters are glued on the cardboard they must be reversed. If a student forgets and the letter prints backwards, he can correct it by simply peeling it off the cardboard and gluing the opposite side down. Now they can print a class quote or a line from a poem on butcher paper using these letters while you explain the idea of movable type and the invention of the printing press. The students will see that certain letters are used more often than others because some get to print their letters more often—these letters are vowels.

If you are using a block of wood for the plate, it can be inked on a common rubber stamp pad. However, the cardboard backing is too difficult for most children to press into the pad because of an inadequate gripping surface, so printing ink and brayer should be used.

The brown bag makes a fine surface for collage, front, back, then opened up to use the sides as well. Two- or three-fold paper cuttings, as described in Polish Paper Cutting, provide attractive symmetrical designs. It is also possible to work directly on the bag, making a scene using fringe and foliage and figures of colored construction paper.

This bag may be used at Halloween as a trick-or-treat bag, at Hanukkah, May Day, Christmas, Cinco de Mayo, or Valentine's Day—the motif fitting the occasion. If it will be tied around the top with yarn, keep the design on the lower half; otherwise, use the whole bag.

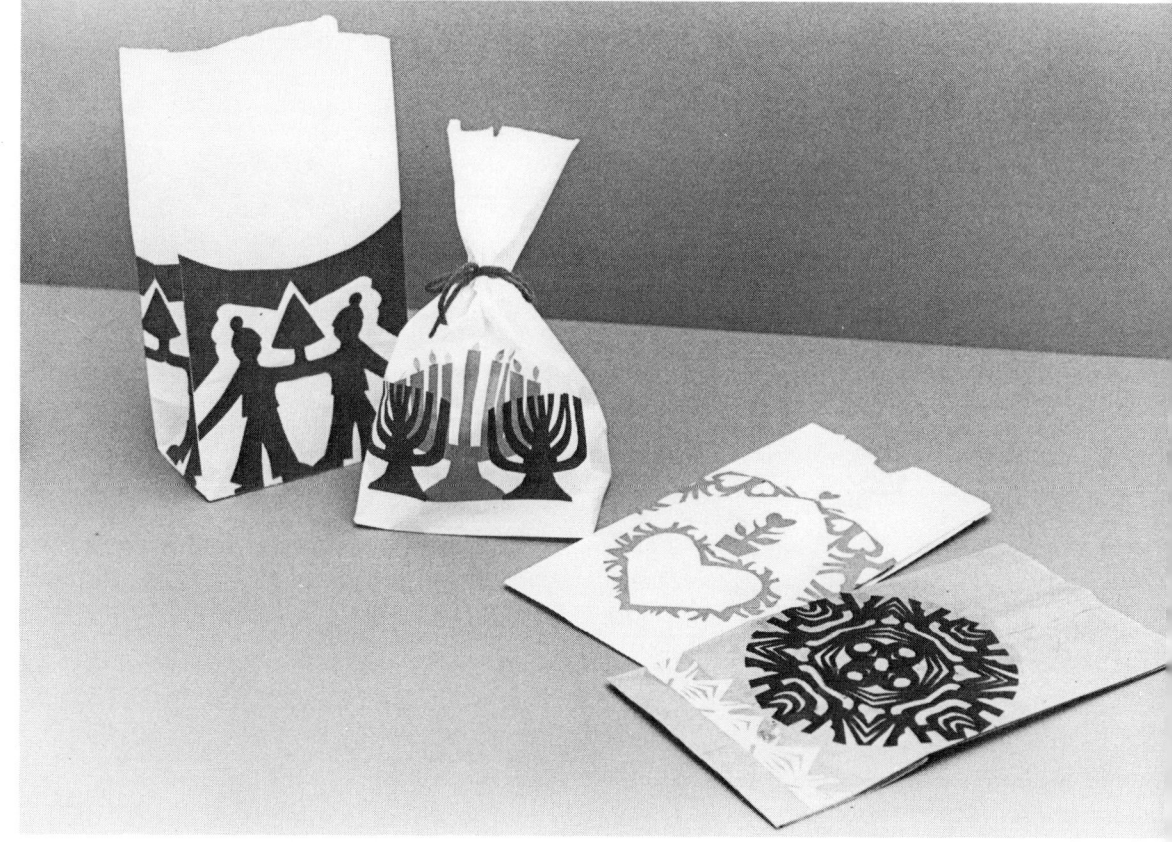

Chop Marks on Paper

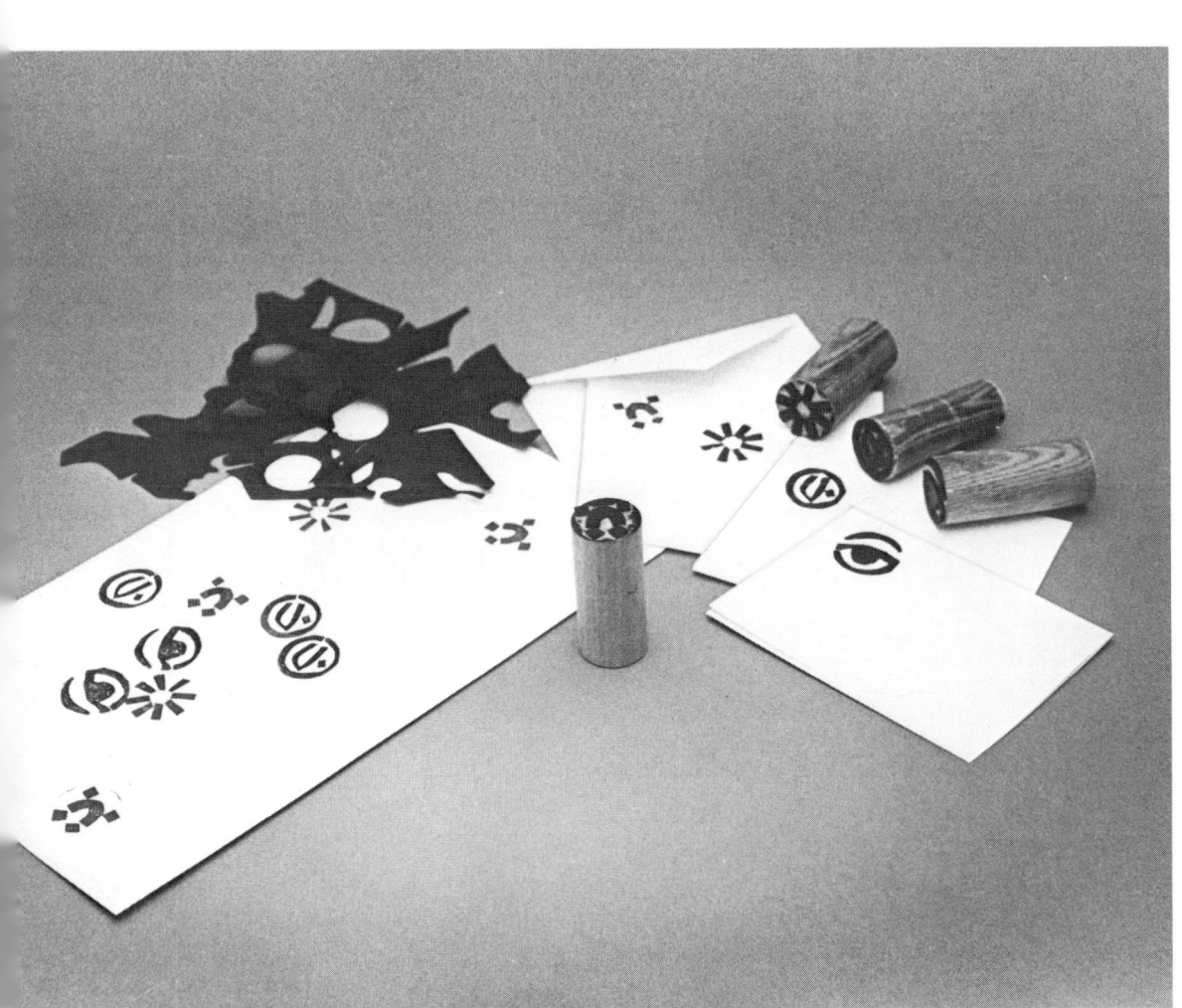

MATERIALS
- Innertube
- Scissors
- Dowel rods 1" in diameter or old broom handles cut in 1" slices
- Newsprint cut in 6" × 9" pieces
- A rubber stamp pad

BOOKS
- S. and B. Epstein, *The First Book of Printing* (Franklin Watts, Inc.).
- Matsuya, *Japanese Design Motifs* (Dover).

INTERRELATING
- Social studies—oriental history of chop marks and Japanese crest designs

NEW VOCABULARY
- chops
- family crests
- emblem

PROCEDURE (3)

A compatible activity to innertube printing on paper is creating a chop mark.

Centuries ago in the Far East, members of the royal families, the court, and other wealthy persons had personal signatures designed for themselves that took the form of wood blocks not larger than 1" square, similar to our rubber stamps. These *chop marks* were inked and stamped on possessions to show ownership. If you look closely at a very old oriental painting or print you will doubtless find many chop marks placed in carefully considered locations, identifying all past owners.

Some of the "chops" were a composite of Chinese characters that conveyed the family name or an expression of a quality associated with its name. Chop marks were also used in the Chinese mercantile system: they were stamped on crates and bundles of goods to indicate their nature and quality.

The Japanese family crests are, in a sense, related to the chops and date back to the eleventh century when the ruling Fujiwara family encouraged the use of an emblem to represent each family name. Some 300 to 500 such designs were made for this purpose. They usually depicted animals, abstract shapes, plants, or natural phenomena. They were used on flags, costumes, weapons, and screens. Some say this was the forerunner of our western trademark, because families engaging in business used their product as a basis for the crest design.

Students can make their own round chop marks with designs cut from innertube and mounted on slices of dowel rod or old broom handles cut into 1" long pieces. Designing a personal logo is a challenge to students because its form must tell about the person as well as identify him. In the West we tend to do such things with initials. This is acceptable, but a design for a chop gives the student an opportunity to use his personal interests for subject matter; for example, a nature lover might use a plant or flower motif; a sports lover, a wheel or a grouping of baseball, football, and tennis ball; a swimmer, waves, or a sprinter, running legs.

Give each student a piece of paper about 6" × 9" on which to draw four or five circles by outlining their dowel or broom handle slice. Have them cut out various shapes or objects to scale from pieces of black construction paper (these can be scraps) and experiment with placement until a design evolves that pleases them. Then, cut the innertube, duplicating the paper shapes, glue it on the end of the dowel, let it dry, and print. They can use these "chops" to sign art work and other papers, which is still a widespread practice in the East.

Cutting Paper

MATERIALS
- Colored construction paper
- Colored magazine pages
- Scissors
- Elmer's glue or glue sticks
- Origami paper (optional)

BOOKS
- Temko, *Paper—Folded, Cut, Sculpted* (Macmillan).
- Bodger, *Paper Dreams* (Universe Books).
- Jablonski, *The Paper Cut-Out Design Book* (Stemmer House).
- Newman, *Paper as Art and Craft* (Crown Publishers).

INTERRELATING
- Social studies—paper art reflecting culture of other countries, principally Poland and Mexico

PURPOSE
- Develop individual decision-making ability
- Manipulate colors and shapes
- Strengthen manual dexterity and small motor control by paper folding and cutting
- Extend measuring skills

NEW VOCABULARY
- Wycinanki (vee-chee-non-kee)
- double and triple fold

PROCEDURE (1–3)

Learning about people through their art gives us many clues about their culture, how they do things, and how they think. Although they may seem quite different from each other and from us at first, investigation of their folk art reveals much we have in common.

Paper cutting is an art form found around the world and reflects social, economic, and religious convictions. The Mexican and Polish traditions we will investigate involve considerable folding before cutting, producing repeated units in a pattern. The Chinese and Swiss tend to cut figures and nature scenes from one flat paper surface. These are unbelievably intricate, executed by people who spend years learning the craft.

Polish Paper Cutting

Moving East from Europe in the nineteenth century, the use of paper spread to Poland into sheep farming areas. One of the farm jobs was shearing sheep, an art in itself. The men were adept at this, sponsoring competitions to decide who could shear a sheep in the shortest time with the highest yield of wool. During the long winter evenings the women, using the same shears, cut designs to amuse the children or perhaps for decoration. These colorful medalions and floral patterns called *Wycinanki* (vee-chee-non-kee) were glued flat to the wall along the ceiling edge and along the sides of the wooden beams; they were also used on chests, chairbacks, and cupboards. Bird and flower motifs were cut and mounted in

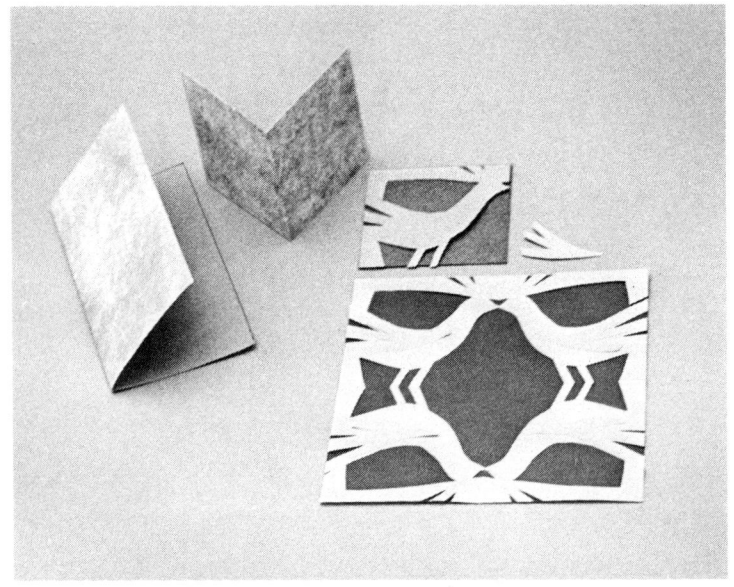

April to celebrate the coming of spring. The precision and delicacy of the designs attracted collectors and can now be found all over the world.

In Polish cutting, the components of a design are cut separately, then assembled and glued on a second sheet of paper. The typical flowers, leaves, and birds are individually cut shapes, moving from the largest and darkest in color on the bottom through several layers to the smallest and lightest on the top. In this way, multicolor effects are achieved. Origami paper is fine for this because it is thin enough for easy folding and cutting and the various colors are bright. If it is unavailable, a fairly solid-colored magazine page can be substituted. Colored construction paper can be used but is recommended only for double, not triple fold cutting.

First have the students try a double fold cut (four repeats), which is good for both square and circular designs. Always begin with a square of paper; if it is not square, fold on the diagonal and cut off the excess. Fold this square in half, then into quarters. Draw a design on the quarter sheet and, to insure fewer mistakes, pencil in the areas to be cut out. Cut carefully and unfold just as carefully so as not to tear the paper.

After the students open the double fold cut, have them decide where they would like to place some spots of color. Choose a second color, duplicate several of the forms in the design, reduce them slightly in size, then glue a series of these forms on top of the original. Straight geometrical forms are also effective. Try cutting three

triangles of three colors in graduated sizes. Glue them, one on top of another, then glue the stack to the basic cutting. This can set up a color vibration or suggest depth through color sequence. It is an opportunity for playful color investigation. Children should move and rearrange colors and shapes several times before making a final decision, thus gaining practice in selecting and choosing.

For mounting, have the children attach the finished design to a second colored sheet. Apply glue to the center area of the paper cutting, position it, and press down for a good bond. When dry, place several spots of glue around the outside edges or corners and press again. This step by step method avoids the frustration of wrinkled or torn paper and shifting parts. The second sheet may in turn be glued to a larger sheet of a third color. The process enhances the original cutting and develops measuring skills.

For a triple fold, have the students start with a square folded in a double fold then folded a third time on the diagonal, transforming the square into a triangle. Proceed as for the double fold. As previously suggested, thin paper is easiest to use for this. Construction paper folded this many times is almost impossible for an adult to cut, certainly for a child. The dip and dye tissue paper described in the chapter on Pattern makes a beautiful cut paper medalion. The tissue may be colored either before or after the cutting. If it is to be dyed after unfolding, dip to edges and cross folds that may be made at will across any section of the wedge. These medalions are very effective inserted between two pieces of Saran Wrap and mounted against the classroom windows.

Mexican Paper Cutting

The Mayans used a kind of paper made from the bark of the fig tree as early as A.D. 500. Later, the Aztecs made paper from cactus for their sacred books and clothing called *amatyl*. The Otomi Indians still produce it. The tribal shamans cut silhouette figures representing a variety of good and bad spirits to use in their religious ceremonies. They also cut another kind of single fold figure, called *El Papel y Las Supersticiones*, from three or four layers of different colored tissue paper and sew it together at various points. Each color represents a particular crop; these figures are placed in the fields to assure an abundant yield. They were first seen by the Franciscan friar Diego de Mendozo in 1569 on a trip to the crater lakes of Nevado de Toluca, where they had been placed in the mountains as sacrifices.

This single fold is much simpler than the double and triple fold of Polish cutting. Since a picture is often worth a thousand words, do a quick demonstration. Fold a piece of paper once, then, holding it so the fold is vertical, cut a zigzag line from top to bottom. Open it up so the students can see the mirror image. The students can cut a figure, animal, flower, tree, abstract shape, or whatever, following the same method. These mirror-image shapes can be mounted on a colorful magazine page background, used with blueprint paper to create a handsome print (see ozalid process), or made into an invitation or holiday greeting card. By glueing one of these positive images on one side of a piece of colored construction paper or cardboard and its remaining background cutout (sometimes called the negative shape) to the flip side of the same cardboard and attaching a string, you have one component for a mobile. When this turns in the wind a provocative positive-negative related image evolves.

It is a good idea to consider the throwaways from cut-and-paste. We ignore these shapes unless someone calls our attention to the fact that they can be more beautiful than the positive shapes. Occasionally, do a small collage with the leftovers. It's a form of recycling that calls for inventive thinking and arranging. Such an exercise may help children form affirmative attitudes toward recycling.

Equation Necklaces

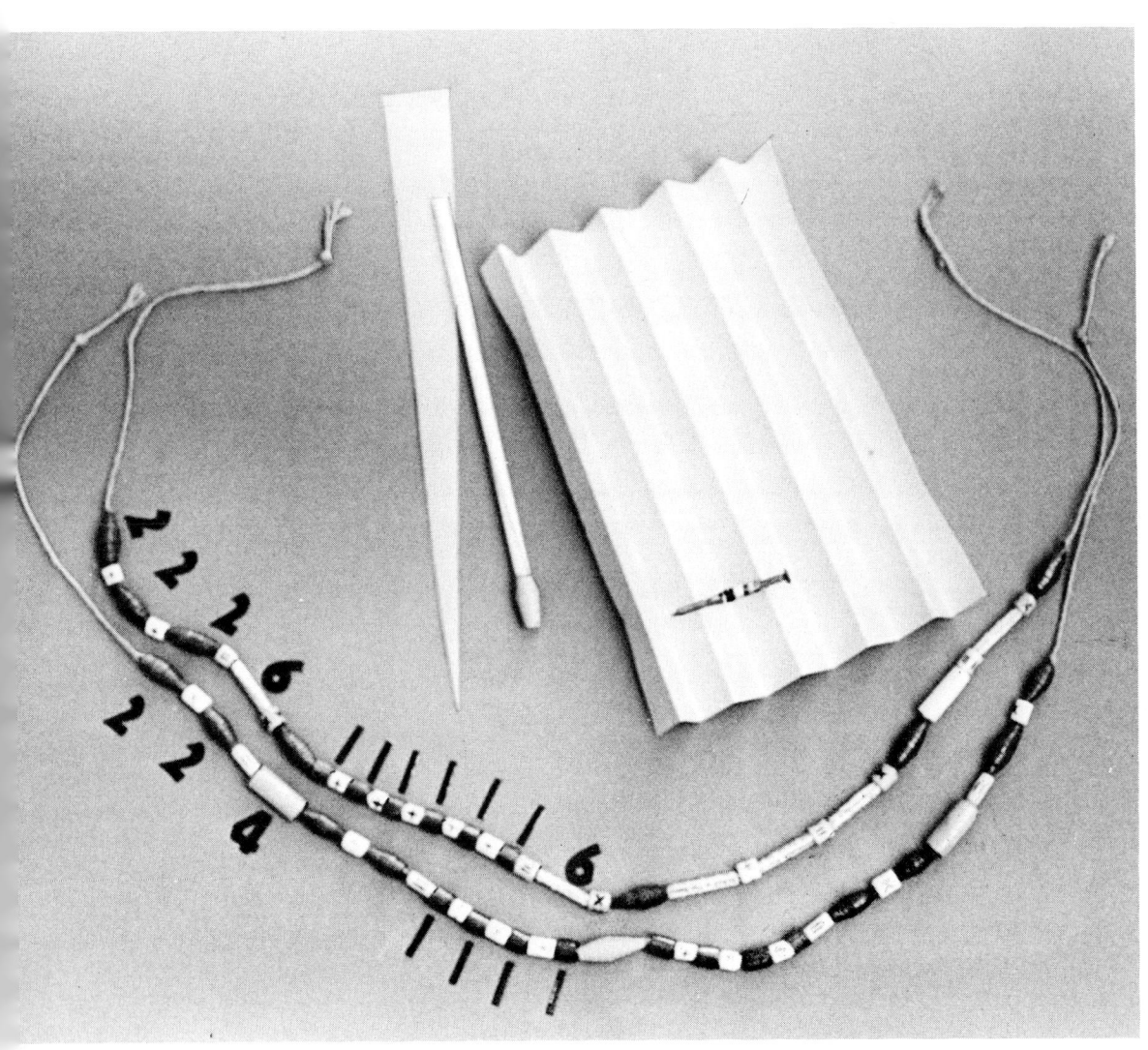

MATERIALS
- Colored construction paper
- Elmer's glue
- String
- Scissors
- Brushes
- Straws
- Rulers
- Used paper (could be old dittos) for recycling
- Waterproof felt-tip markers

BOOKS
- Nuffield Mathematics Project, *Computation and Structure* (John Wiley).
- Baratta-Lorton, *Mathematics Their Way* (Addison-Wesley).

INTERRELATING

Math through exploration of addition and multiplication facts and patterns

PURPOSE

- Find different solutions to one problem
- Explore multiplication in terms of relationships and commutative skills
- Reinforce counting and addition skills
- Relate real objects to an abstract idea
- Manipulate concrete materials into symmetrical patterns

NEW VOCABULARY

worry beads	recycle
abacus	parallel
computer	random pattern
equation	

PROCEDURE (3)

Beads have a long history. They have been used as adornment and decoration since early Egyptian time, as money in numerous primitive tribes, and as trade counters in Africa and among various Indian tribes. They have been used for counting prayers and as "worry" beads to keep apprehensive and tense Greek fingers occupied. Beads on an abacus comprised the original computer. We're going to use them for reviewing addition and multiplication and, perhaps, as trade beads.

Beads can be made from many kinds of paper. Colored construction paper is a good choice for beginners: it's readily available, easy to control, and makes an impressive bead. After the students have a work session to become acquainted with the process and the paper properties required to make good bead material, start a friendly competition to find unique kinds of paper for the activity. Have students bring their collections to school, and share them if possible. Wallpaper samples, brown grocery bags, newspapers, magazine pages, and junk mail are just a few suggestions. Thin magazine pages make narrow beads; thick wallpaper makes wide beads.

A basic bead is made by rolling a long triangle of paper over a straw, nail, knitting needle, or toothpick. The nail and knitting needle may be too hard for elementary students to pull out of the bead after wrapping; the toothpick will make a hole too small for them to push a needle and thread through. A fail-safe selection is the straw, wrapped with paper and left in the bead. Children can drop thread through its center and pull it out the other side without a needle.

For kindergarteners, you should provide the paper triangles already cut. From first grade up, have the students cut at least some of their own. It's very good small muscle coordination practice.

If the students are cutting their own triangles, have them turn the construction paper so the length is horizontal. Measure and mark 1″ segments down one edge of the paper, starting from the top. On the opposite edge, mark ½″ down, then proceed with the 1″ segmentation to the bottom. Draw a line from the top corner of the first side to the ½″ mark from the top on the opposite side, then from the ½″ mark back to the next inch mark on the opposite side. Continue until the page is covered with triangles created by this zigzag line pattern. This is an efficient use of paper—not a bit is wasted. The two odd cuts on either long end will make smaller beads.

Wrap the wide end of the paper snugly around one end of the straw and roll, keeping the tension constant. This takes a bit of practice but students usually catch on quickly because they want to make beads. When the paper is all wound on, put enough Elmer's glue on the tip end to fasten it down. Hold it for a few seconds until the glue sets (if a little oozes out it's all right because it dries transparently). Cut the straw off at the end of the bead and repeat the performance.

When all beads have been wrapped and dried, slip each onto a toothpick or nail for holding while painting them with two parts Elmer's glue mixed with one part water. Set them crosswise between two triangular racks. Each student can make these for himself from used paper: cut the sheet in half, lengthwise, then divide each piece lengthwise into three equal strips and fold accordingly to form two long triangles. When set parallel to each other, the racks can hold the beaded toothpicks or nails, laid between them, allowing the beads to dry without touching each other.

A cylindrical bead provides a second shape and a little variety. It is constructed from a strip of paper of equal width along its entire length, rolled on a straw. Just be careful to keep the edges flush. This bead has the largest surface and is good for students who wish to add designs with waterproof felt-tip markers before painting with glue. Incidentally, this glue coating preserves the bead, deepens the color, and gives it a sheen.

When stringing the beads, be sure to knot the last bead on and leave enough string on either end with which to tie the necklace.

For the math segment of this activity, each student will plan an equation and translate it into color and beading, representing each number by a color. The students will also need several beads with these symbols: ×, =, and +. Cylindrical beads work best. These symbols make fine designs when repeated around the bead with felt-tip pens.

Let's work with beginning multiplication. Using the table, one student picks $2 \times 2 = 4$. He lays out a blue bead, a × bead, a blue bead, an = bead, and a yellow bead (the colors are arbitrary). If he lays beads between the frame of the two long paper triangles they will not roll off the desk. This five-bead set is not enough for a necklace so he must find a second equation that says the same thing in a different way. He chooses $2 \times 2 = 1+1+1+1$, or a blue bead, a × bead, a blue bead, an = bead, a red, a red, a red, and a red, adding eleven beads to the original five, totaling sixteen—enough for a necklace made of construction paper. Take a second equation, $2 \times 3 = 6$, which can be said in these ways: $2 \times 3 = 3 + 3$, or $2 \times 3 = 1 + 1 + 1 + 1 + 1 + 1$, or $2 \times 3 = 2 + 2 + 2$. The first two equations develop a 22-bead pattern, which the student might wish to repeat. By reversing the order the second time, he gets a symmetrical pattern of 44 beads. Between each equation he can use a transitional bead, one quite different from the others, to separate the equations. These beads might be made of newspaper, magazine pages, or some other material, and strung so they hang lengthwise. Laying out the bead patterns and checking them before stringing saves a lot of frustration.

When each child has made a good number of beads, some children may wish to barter; thus they become trade beads.

In this activity, students learn alternative ways of stating multiplication facts, become familiar with them by working with concrete materials, and enjoy the patterns various equations make. Reading each other's necklaces, they learn equations and their multiplication memories are reinforced.

Beading can also be used for addition. Such equations as $4 + 2 = 2 + 4$ repeated four or five times yields a fine pattern, whereas $4 + 2 = 3 + 3 = 5 + 1 = 1 + 1 + 1 + 1 + 1 + 1$ produces an equally fine random pattern. Should it be repeated? Forward or backward or not at all? Placed in two rows? The student can decide after seeing it in tangible form and perhaps looking at other students' sequences.

This activity can also be used just for the purpose of experimenting with colors, textures, and various ways of stringing beads for effect.

Wax-Dipped Forms

MATERIALS
    Colored construction paper
    Colored tissue paper
    Elmer's glue or glue sticks
    Pencils
    Rulers
    Spool of nylon thread and needles
    An old metal pan
    Hot plate
    Three packages of paraffin (at the grocery store)
    Scissors
    A length of heavy string for a clothes line

PURPOSE
    Explore color combinations
    Follow a sequence of directions
    Learn safety precautions
    Exercise responsibility for each other

NEW VOCABULARY
    sandwich between frames
    paraffin
    hot plate

PROCEDURE (2–3)

    Pass out two pieces of 6" × 9" colored construction paper (cut one 9" × 12" piece in half) to each student. Have them place one sheet on top of the other and fold them together, lengthwise, being careful to keep the edges together. Each should hold his folded paper so the open edges are on the right and the fold is on the left (reverse for left-handers). Draw a margin line 1" in from the edge, across the top, down the side with the open

edges, and across the bottom. Starting from the folded edge, cut a shape, being careful not to cross over the margin line. Second- and third-graders can cut two separate shapes, one above the other, if they wish. Now, open the fold and you have two identical frames with a cutout in the center. Next, cut colored or dip-dye tissue larger than the holes but smaller than 6" × 9". Glue the tissue over the window, close the other half of the frame over it, and glue the frames together; the tissue is now sandwiched between the two frames. If the students did cut two separate shapes, they might wish to use two colors of tissue. This takes more careful cutting and pasting.

Have some students help you spread newspaper on the floor under string clothes line, strung between a couple of heavy tables or chairs, about table-height, six or more feet long. Other students can cut nylon thread into 12" lengths, enough for the class. Each student will thread it through a large-eyed needle, sew through the top center of the frame, and tie it to one end of the thread.

In a deep fat fryer or metal pan and hot plate, melt some paraffin to a depth of 4". A small hot plate will do the job nicely. Keep it hot enough for the paraffin to remain transparent but not so hot that it will smoke. For easy clean-up, place newspapers under this pan and along the path to the clothes line.

This activity presents an opportunity to talk about safety precautions, taking turns, and being responsible for each other. These points are especially applicable when the students line up for the "big dipping"—the highlight of the activity. Something about this operation pleases them no end as each one, holding the end of his thread, dips his tissue form under the warm wax, lifts it up, and lets the excess wax drip into the pan for a second or two before carrying it to the clothes line. He ties it on the line to dry and cool, which takes about five minutes.

The paraffin gives depth to the color and a transparency to the tissue, reminiscent of stained glass. Although most paper will fade if exposed to strong light over a period of time, the color in this paper is protected by the wax surfacing.

These tissue forms can be hung by their strings in a cluster from the ceiling or placed side by side, wide and high, against a window to form a striking overall design, bringing unexpected color and lift to the classroom.

If there is time for the students to make a second form, and they will want to once they know the technique, they can work with shape and color relationships. Also, with two in hand, they may be more inclined to let you keep one for display.

Papier-Mâché Fruit and Vegetables

MATERIALS
- Newspaper
- Dishpan
- Assorted fruits and vegetables
- Wallpaper paste
- Tempera paint and recycled latex paint
- Brushes
- Magazines
- Elmer's glue
- Shellac (optional)

BOOKS
See Monster Mâché

INTERRELATING
Health sciences—using finished shapes for activities teaching nutrition

PURPOSE
Observe the process of duplication using fruit and vegetables as molds

PROCEDURE (1–3)
Papier-mâché is an amazingly versatile process that can be made simple enough for kindergarten children (see Monster Mâché) or as complex and refined as an adult might wish. It is ideal for three-dimensional work in the school because it is cheap, strong, and light-weight when dry. The surface used for the stripping process can be chickenwire, hardware cloth, crumpled newspaper, or

an actual object, to mention just a few. Fruit or vegetables provide an ideal base because they are large enough for students to avoid tedious detail, yet small enough that they can complete at least one piece each. Examples of good fruit bases are apples, oranges, pears, and bananas; vegetable bases could be carrots, onions, and potatoes. These are all reasonably smooth and strips can be applied easily.

Follow the directions given in Monster Mâché for mixing the paste, but tear the newspaper strips in 1" widths and 2" lengths. Rubbing the fruit or vegetables with Vaseline before stripping facilitates its removal from the completed mâché. Apply two layers of strips, making sure all edges and puckers are pressed down. Use black and white newspaper for the first layer and colored newsprint for the second. This makes the layers easy to see.

When finished, the pieces should be placed in the sun or in a warm place in the room until dry. Apply two more layers in the same way. *You* do the next step: using a single-edge razor blade, encircle the round shapes with a cut-line simulating their equators. If the fruit or vegetable is longer than it is wide (a banana or carrot), the cut-line should be lengthwise and continue all the way around. The mâché can easily be separated into two parts, which will pull right off the base. If the base fruit or vegetable is not damaged it can be used again. Place the two parts together and apply two layers of papier-mâché over the seam, let it dry, then strip it with a final layer, carefully covering all bumps and blemishes. When dry, the fruit can be painted realistically or with colorful designs. Children can decorate it with a collage of colored tissue or torn shapes from magazine pages. What else can the class suggest?

These finished shapes may be used in a variety of activities dealing with food and nutrition.

MATERIALS
Ozalid or blueprint paper
5″ × 8″ sheet of plastic or glass (size approximate)
Ammonia
Two or three plastic dishpans
Collected natural or man-made objects

INTERRELATING
Science—examining the effect of the sunlight on various paper surfaces

PURPOSE
Learn a printing process induced by light
Experiment with process variations to achieve effects
Explore timing sequences

NEW VOCABULARY
ozalid
blueprint paper
emulsion

PROCEDURE (2-3)

The ozalid blueprint has been around for a long time but each new group of children coming into K−3 seems to enjoy it as much as the last. It is a distant relative of the photographic process. When paper is coated with diazo emulsion and exposed to light, the emulsion burns

off down to the bare paper, which turns from its original color to white. Any covered portion of the paper retains the emulsion, which is then fixed permanently by an ammonia and water solution.

Ozalid blueprint or other inexpensive reproducing papers can be purchased from any drafting supply house. The smallest size available is 8½" × 11". You can cut it in half to 8½" × 5½" in a darkened room; it will still provide adequate surface for printing. The sheets should be kept in a closed envelope until immediately before use.

Start with a piece of cardboard, a magazine, or a board of some sort that will act as a firm support for the sheet of blueprint. Place the flat object or cutout shape to be printed on top of the paper and cover it with a piece of glass or clear plastic. This holds the shape flat and immobile against the surface. Then expose the paper to sunlight for several minutes until the surface turns from blue to almost white. Immediately, run the print through a sequence of solutions set up in three dishpans, the first containing water, the second one part ammonia to two parts water and the third water again. Place the print on newspaper. It will tend to buckle, so place the print under a stack of heavy books to dry. Students will be pleased with the finished prints as they stand but they can also add color shapes cut from construction paper, colored line, or simple mats, as outlined in Exhibitions. This process also works well with natural forms and gadgets as printing material. It invites experimentation because so many variables exist; subject matter, timing, sequential movement during exposure, and a combination of natural and cut-out materials are just a few. It is good practice to plan the arrangement on a practice paper the approximate size of the ozalid, then transfer the arrangement to the blueprint paper. The process must go quickly once the paper is exposed to light.

SECTION IV
The Purpose of Education in the Arts

About Perceiving

Perception, or how we know, and knowledge, what we know about, are closely related and affect each other deeply.

Our perception is influenced by our knowledge. If this knowledge is limited and flawed, we will perceive the world as limited and flawed. If our perception is to become more discerning of the existence, nature, and identity of all things surrounding us, it must be supported by an enlightened and continually expanding body of information.

Reverse this proposal and it is still correct—our knowledge is influenced by our perception. If we perceive the circumstances in which knowledge is presented as purposeful and positive, we become responsive and capable. Should we perceive them as threatening or pointless, then fear or distrust virtually terminates receptiveness regardless of how valuable the information may be.

So it is with the child. If he perceives his school environment—particularly his teacher—as concerned about his well-being and learning, he will be receptive and consequently more capable than he would be in an atmosphere of insecurity. Learning results from a delicate mix of the intellectual and the intuitive, the analytical and the relational, the sequential and the multiple.

A whole, perceptive human being, a balance of the two, is education's goal.

Methods of Sculpture—Additive and Subtractive

Shaping perception and expanding knowledge is a little like building a piece of sculpture. Some artists believe there are two ways of making a three-dimensional shape in space: one is the additive method, and the other, the subtractive. Looking back over several thousand years of art history, we can see the subtractive method is far and away the favorite of early sculptors. It fit the materials at hand—stone and marble. It nurtured the monolith, a vertical shape puncturing space like a huge needle, "undifferentiated, massive and consequently rigid and unyielding in its attributes," according to the dictionary. Take any obelisk as an example, better yet, take any pharoah sitting on his throne or standing frozen with hands at his side, single and solid. The stone figure supports itself. Its shape is its strength: wide and heavy at the bottom, earthbound. It tapers up to a narrow head with no penetrations or openings anywhere in the form. Much later, in Greece, a genius like Praxiteles happened along, finding ways to deviate from the single-column syndrome by manipulating open spaces between the figure parts, and suggesting action or movement. Even so, a limited number of things can be said or done with a monolith. This subtractive method requires working from the outside in, beginning with a block of marble and subtracting chip after chip to free the shape within.

Michelangelo used the subtractive method. When beginning a work, he had a reasonable idea of how his finished figure should look. He spent a good deal of time selecting the exact size and kind of marble slab to accommodate his vision. This genius chiseled life into his figures in spite of the restrictions of the material.

In contrast, the artist using the additive method works from the inside out. He begins with an open framework or skeleton of metal or wood called an *armature*. He then adds his material, a little at a time, layer on layer, to this armature, reinforcing the form and allowing the shape to r-e-a-c-h o-u-t and penetrate space with almost unlimited freedom.

Additive sculpture probably developed from the introduction of new materials. Strong, fresh directions in the arts have often resulted from the discovery of a material that allows the artist to think new thoughts and give form to ideas previously held captive in his mind for want of an appropriate material for expression. The same thing happens in the classroom. A new material or novel combination of known materials can prove irresistible to a student, even spark a whole class into passionate activity and original application.

A contemporary artist working in the additive fashion begins with an idea but does not particularly outline the finished image. In this way, he is free to observe the piece as it grows and changes and watch shapes and ideas evolve, playing against and influencing one another. He can take advantage of any innovation or revelation presenting itself during the process and incorporate it into the work if he chooses. Obviously, he cannot possibly preconceive the final form. The process itself is stimulating and full of surprises.

Learning Compared to Sculpting

In the classroom, the child learns to perceive and to know in ways closely approximating either the subtractive or additive method of shaping sculpture. During the first years of a child's education, if the learning experiences do not allow him to make genuine discoveries on his own, followed by analysis, evaluation, and discussion, he may perceive of knowledge as a huge monolithic body of preselected information—intimidating and impersonal. He has little notion how to incorporate immediate experience into this rigid structure or how to deeply penetrate its form. At the end of his school career he may have digested most of this mass of information, finding it occasionally intriguing but frozen and unyielding in the presence of new possibilities. He will also find much of it outdated.

Shaping perception and knowledge the additive way, however, means working from the inside out. The teacher gives the student some responsibility for his own growth by presenting alternatives from which the student alone can choose. Then, as he discovers and learns new ideas, he layers them on to his armature of principles and convictions, replacing the outgrown and inferior with the more enlightened and substantial. The process is open and free enough to allow him to r-e-a-c-h o-u-t and express what is real for him with almost unlimited freedom. This process sustains a constant state of growth, colored by positive expectations, and thus fulfils John Dewey's definition of education as "the continuous reconstruction of experience which adds to the meaning of experience and increases the ability to direct the course of subsequent experience."

About Learning

If the rate of general change over the last ten years is any indication of things to come, only an infallible clairvoyant would venture a description of the world of 1985–95. Yet, we claim to be educating our children for it. Much of this education follows old, safe patterns.

PREPARATION FOR THE FUTURE

How can we best prepare children for this future? What lasting values can we help them develop? There is no doubt we're in an educational revolution over these questions. We have tried open schools and free schools; we have private and public schools. We have traditional and structured approaches to teaching as well as nonstructured and far-out experimental classrooms. The number of books published in the fields of eucational psychology, methodology, and philosophy escalates. And, since no change is likely to occur until controversy and debate demand it, this activity has its affirmative side. But somewhere amid all the concern and rhetoric the child and his needs are often lost.

WAYS OF KNOWING:
COGNITIVE AND AFFECTIVE

To function in this world the student must learn to read, write, verbalize, and compute. These skills are usually taught in a logical and sequential way to prepare the student to comprehend, and ultimately evaluate, his experiences. This way of knowing—traditionally the goal of educators—is basic to the cognitive domain as outlined in Bloom's *Taxonomy of Educational Objectives, Handbook I: Cognitive Domain*.

A second way of knowing, the affective, involves attitudes, commitment, and the organization of a value system; it is described in *Taxonomy of Educational Objectives, Handbook II: Affective Domain*, by Krathwohl, Bloom, and Masia. The cognitive way of knowing, central to the educational system until recently, has been utilized to the detriment and often exclusion of the affective domain. However, the competent teacher, knowing the importance of attitude and commitment to learning of any kind, balances the two domains.

STRUCTURING UNDERSTANDING

What potential benefit would come of combining both processes? Consider a student who applies his reading and observation skills to tracing a few of man's historical accomplishments. He can memorize the written facts and examine the artifacts of a period but they will have no real meaning for him unless someone leads him to make relational connections. However, through direct discussion the student can comprehend that these accomplishments were influenced by the cultural, spiritual, economic, and geographical conditions of their times; that needs, and sometimes fortuitous events, make demands that force innovation. This can have direct application to his life, and therein lies its real meaning for him.

Suppose he is reading of the Sung Dynasty, roughly 900 B.C. to A.D. 1200, a high point in Chinese culture. During this period Chinese ceramic art was refined to produce superbly beautiful porcelain. He sees photographs of pots and bowls that look at least as good as those he sees today, 2,000 years later. Their secret was closely guarded for hundreds of years. A few pieces were brought back to Europe in the crusades. There, royalty, accustomed to eating from gold or silver plates, considered the heavy earthenware ceramics they knew to be fit only for peasants. They went wild over the exquisitely thin, translucent, white oriental porcelain. Charles VII of France, in 1447, asked the Sultan of Babylon for just one piece because of its rarity. In 1566, Queen Elizabeth owned only two pieces. Europe took another 200 years to discover the secret. These are cold historical facts. However, the student who has been guided to develop his sensitivity and intuition—affective values—will ask himself why it happened in China at that particular time. Investigation will show him that the wealthy imperial court, sophisticated and intellectual, valued the arts and commissioned or commanded artists and craftsmen to create objects for use in religious ceremonies and court decoration. So we have cultural, spiritual, and economic conditions bringing about the desire for new forms. Geography played its part by providing kaolin, a white clay, which, mixed with other clay bodies and fired, results in this ware with its elegant paper-thin walls and tough practical surface. Kaolin is mainly found in three places in the world—China, Georgia, and North Carolina—and nothing much was going on in the latter two at the time. The making of procelain in China in A.D. 1000 was a grand concidence of time, place, and circumstances.

As the student, again and again, is led to discover connections between human needs (circumstances) and invention (response), first in subjects he studies then in his own life, he begins to recognize patterns. He begins to infer and predict. He begins to think for himself. In addition, when he moves from one content area or experience to another, either in or out of school, this thought processing helps him confront what at first may seem unfamiliar by searching out elements he can relate to his past experience and accumulated knowledge. Although he may only sense these elements, they provide a basis for proceeding. Otherwise he would have none.

RECENT RESEARCH

Educators' growing recognition of the affective values that can be developed so significantly through the arts is partially due to the considerable recent research about the two hemispheres of the brain, each with its own affective component but differing widely in cognitive information-processing ability. The left hemisphere performs intellectual, digital, and rational functions and dominates verbalization, reading, calculating, and writing skills. The right hemisphere performs intuitive, analogic, and metaphoric functions and dominates the kinesthetic and visual—imagery, the relational, and the integral. U. Neisser in his book, *Cognitive Psychology*, calls them sequential and multiple processing abilities, respectively. By "multiple" he means the ability to carry out "many actions simultaneously or at least independently." Dr. J. E. Bogen, a pioneer in hemispheric research, writes, "we can see that an elementary school program narrowly restricted to reading, writing and arithmetic will educate mainly one hemisphere, leaving half of an individual's high level potential unschooled." And, "it means that the entire student body is being educated lopsidedly." If education is to prepare thoughtful, totally functioning individuals, rationality and sensitivity must be given equal time. Robert Samples, writing in *The Metaphoric Mind*, suggests a "balanced blend of rationality and intuition, of linearity and metaphor, of digital and analogic functions" and adds, "intuitive, analogic and metaphoric functions are patently ignored in today's schooling." The arts foster intuitive, analogic, and metaphoric thinking. They draw heavily on images, emotions, imagination, and invention.

FREE PLAY OF IDEAS

A good art session guides the student to observe, explore, speculate, and manipulate ideas and materials. It provides time for fooling around with possibilities just for the joy of it. This method is basic training for the independent spirit; it means juggling a number of nonspecific alternatives—multiple processing—before making a decision. Such free play invites something spontaneous and creative to happen. Students are likely to discover some basic relationships and to make analogies, leading to the "eureka moment," that sensation of touching something vast and deep and real through their own efforts. How else will they glimpse the structure and wholeness of things just waiting to be seen? Why else would they venture into untried areas of thought and experience, suspending fear of failure, if not that their previous successes have been so satisfying?

Learning to think in terms of ideas and relationships is a lasting accomplishment basic to all future living and decision-making. This is how education can help prepare students for the future.

COLLAGE ACTIVITY

Let's consider two presentations of the same cut-and-paste art activity at the early elementary level. The purpose is to acquaint the children with body structure, to illustrate that the human figure is made up of a variety of parts that bend and work together. In the first presentation, we tack up on the wall a simplified human figure, with body parts cut from colored paper and mounted on a white paper background. Scissors and paper are distributed. The children copy the model, to the best of their ability, while the teacher points out various proportions, joints, and how they bend. It is assumed that direct copying and assembly of cut paper parts will accomplish the objective. But many children will not see much relationship between themselves and "that picture." If there are 28 children in the class the result will be 28 figures so similar that their most distinguishing features may be the names printed on the paper. This is visual fact and data level processing. However, there is a whole roomful of human figures—why not use them as models instead of a paper figure?

EXPLORATION RATHER THAN IMITATION

In the second presentation, colored construction paper, scissors, and paste are set out. The children select their own colors. They are guided to observe various parts of their own bodies and how they relate to each other, their dimensions, how they bend, and how they connect. This is a good time to do some body movement activities to learn about proportions. Are legs longer or shorter than arms? Working with partners, the children can measure and compare. Are feet longer or shorter than hands? The students must interact, compare and make decisions. The three-dimensional figures they are working with are their own bodies.

Some young children will draw short arms growing out of either side of a huge head unless they have reason to look and see where the arms are actually attached. One approach might be for you to ask the artist to scratch his knee with his finger. He does it. Then ask if his picture-figure can do the same thing. He should see that the arms are too short. This is also a good time to point out that the elbow bends in the middle of the arm and allows freedom of movement. It may take several sessions before the children can grasp these ideas.

The second approach, covering the same cognitive materials as the first, allows children to grasp and remember information because they are actively involved in their own learning. Some of the time they are even teaching each other. Twenty-eight different statements extend the cut-and-paste skill to a level of individual learning and expression. The skill, cut-and-paste, becomes a mechanism through which children disclose their insights.

Results of the second venture, although loaded with new meaning for the child, may baffle parents and sometimes the teacher. Since the child has been encouraged to rely on his own observation and decisions, his product is rarely slick and finished-looking, but it is a record of his visual thinking—a point of view quite different from that of adults.

Papíer mâché sculpture by the author

About Additional Benefits of Learning Through the Arts

As a child works through subject area skills and principles, he concurrently develops qualities of mind and spirit that shape his emerging character. If what is being taught is substantial and usable, intellectual growth and character development occur simultaneously.

Desirable qualities, if they are to mature and deepen, must be stimulated. Responsibility, resourcefulness, integrity cannot be developed in ways that separate them from experience. We can read about, define, and examine them, but we must also feel and express them if we are to understand them.

Each of the following sections describes how working in the arts strengthens affirmative qualities in the child's character while expanding his ability to see, to feel, and to think.

LEARNING THROUGH THE ARTS REQUIRES MAKING AND DOING

Children learn by doing. Webster's definition of art is "making and doing things that have form and beauty"—not particularly sonatas or paintings or sculpture, but things, any things that have form and beauty. The arts require children to be participants, not spectators.

Making and doing in the arts puts the child in touch with his attitudes and emotions, with himself. Since objective self-appraisal does not take place by isolating the self but rather by defining it in context, in relation to others, it forces the restricting limitations of a narrow ego to give way. The child begins to perceive of himself as an individual part of a large and active whole. This perception has a great deal to do with how he sees others.

The emphasis art places on individuality and thoughtful diversity assures each child that he has something to contribute to the whole. He is needed. He has a place in the scheme of things. Children need to support one another and this can happen naturally in the arts. Few of the child's other daily activities suggest to him that his uniqueness is precious, that it can be maintained in a group situation, or that, if properly channeled, it can even strengthen the group-whole.

Making and doing together gives children an appreciation of the problems involved in group activity, as well as a basis for judgement and an eye for genuine accomplishment. It brings children closer to one another because they are participating in a common experience and learning together. Thus, the child gains a fuller sense of identity from getting to know himself in context, a sense of purpose from being a contributing part of a whole, and a sense of fulfillment from combining the two. Identity, purpose, and fulfillment are basic human needs and require constant tender encouragement.

Children must make and do, often. No talent ever developed without practice. Charles Olson, the American poet, says, "... nothing is possible without doing it. It is where the test lies, malgré all the thought and all the pell mell of proposing it. Or thinking it out or living it ahead of time."*

---

*From Charles Olson, *The Maximus Poems,* Volume III (Grossman Publishers, 1975).

Qualities strengthened: independent thinking
self-awareness
self-reliance
compassion
innovation
cooperation
discernment
observation
willingness to work
self-instruction

LEARNING THROUGH THE ARTS ENCOURAGES CREATIVE THINKING SKILLS

Expanding the child's knowledge of the world is only half of the educator's responsibility—teaching him to use it effectively is equally important. Using knowledge in resourceful and positive ways necessitates cultivating problem-solving and creative-thinking skills.

Much of the children's problem-solving in the classroom is the application of reason in an analytical step-by-step approach. Another method that calls up powerful responses and stretches children's ingenuity is the application of imagination and intuition to problems. Jerome Bruner calls this the training of hunches, the shrewd guess, or the "courageous leap to a tentative conclusion." These, he says, "are the most valuable coin of the thinker at work, whatever his line of work."

Suppose the creative thinker has a problem to solve. He analyzes the situation, collecting all the pertinent and impertinent information that might even remotely apply. Then he takes all this information and pokes it, shuffles it, turns it upside down, inside out, and sideways. He tries to see it in a new context, to break his familiar pattern of perceiving. He is looking for a way to shape these separate possibilities into a form. He makes a shrewd guess or plays a hunch and brings together two or more of these ideas into a new relationship. The Eureka moment! The resolution is a unity, a new form, a new insight. If the problem-solver considers the new form superior to previous ones, he incorporates it into his thinking and acting, and he grows. Problems can force growth and become opportunities in disguise.

Reordering, recombining, and transforming are synonyms for creativity. The New York designer, Milton Glaser, says it this way:

> Let me make a generality about how a designer or an artist works at his best level. The best work emerges from the observation of phenomena that exists independently of each other. What the designer intuits is the linkage singular or plural. He sees a way to unify separate occurrences and to create a gestalt, an experience in which this new unity provides a new insight. It doesn't really matter, in a sense, what the subject matter is...or the means to convey it...what is essential is the perception of the linkage between phenomena. So whatever it is, whether it's time and space or heat and light or you and me...the critical act is to understand the linkages and to bring phenomena that have never been unified into some kind of unity. That's what design is about and what art is about,

and it doesn't really matter what the media considerations are.*

Through practice and frequent application, the urge to recombine and reorder and transform becomes irresistible, a part of our nature. This same kind of thinking is involved in producing a work of art, an invention, a mathematical of scientific theory, or a musical composition. Creativity is not limited to the arts but it can be most clearly developed through them.

Thinking creatively is not a rare gift, not some kind of magic but a thought process worth cultivating that is both self-expanding and self-renewing.

Qualities strengthened: resourcefulness
inquisitiveness
adaptability
invention
analysis
imagination
ingenuity

LEARNING THROUGH THE ARTS INCREASES THE ABILITY TO CONCENTRATE

The morning schedule in many schools is math-to-science-to-language arts in 50-minute modules relieved by an occasional recess. This precision is efficient but learning in such a relentless routine becomes questionable. This can fragment thinking and cause children to form habits of superficial surface exploration. Children need to experience in-depth perceptions and explorations. Why not take advantage of the opportunity the arts offer to expand concentration and self-motivation by presenting an occasional morning combining all the disciplines?

The student who has a science block, who sits back and turns off until that module is over, may be led into science by an integrated approach. Because of the continuity inherent in the process, he will have trouble recognizing where one segment ends and science begins. Enticed by the opening instructions for building a six-foot paper construction, with careful direction he can be into the work and doing well before he realizes it is a detailed model of a windmill for pumping water. After several such adventures he may come to see himself as competent in an integrated approach. And we all like to do what we're good at doing.

Most teachers have had the experience of introducing in the arts, an idea, a material, or a combination of the two that the class found so totally absorbing that experimentation and learning could have continued for hours. During this period, they forgot the pressure of time in the stimulation of complete involvement. Most children slip into the drama and rhythm of the creative experience eagerly and would hardly recognize participation as an exercise in acquiring intellectual tenacity. They learn to concentrate and to focus all their capabilities in one area. Children learn to concentrate by doing it. And doing it. And doing it again.

Qualities strengthened: attentiveness
perseverence

---

*GRAPHIC DESIGN. First published by The Overlook Press, Woodstock, New York 12498. Copyright Milton Glaser 1973.

LEARNING THROUGH THE ARTS SHARPENS THE ABILITY TO MAKE DECISIONS

A creative work is the record of a long series of decisions. The quality of the work—whether a painting, sculpture, drama, dance, or musical composition—depends on the calibre of the choices made during the creative process, just as the quality of our lives depends on the depth of understanding behind our daily decisions. The ability to make appropriate decisions comes with knowledge, and again, with practice. "Even genius," writes Delacroix, "is the gift of generalizing and choosing."

One of the great values of the art experience is that immediate testing of ideas and concepts is possible. In the visual arts, for instance, the appropriateness of a decision is instantly apparent. The painter adding a colored shape to his canvas immediately perceives it in context. Then he asks himself, "Does it work? Does that red compromise with the existing colors or is it too loud and belligerent?" "Is the shape relationship, in terms of size, right? Is there enough space around it for emphasis?" He considers these questions and the alternatives. The answers decide his next step. Each addition to the canvas is the result of an exchange of ideas between the artist and the unfolding work. He is at once artist and critic, and he becomes more discriminating with practice. So it is with the child who is encouraged to work in this way: his confidence and discrimination grow with experience. This ability to analyze, evalute, and select filters into other study areas, increasing his potential for learning enormously.

Qualities stengthened: judgment
responsiveness
spontaneity
confidence
analysis
evaluation
selectivity
perception

LEARNING THROUGH THE ARTS REQUIRES RESOLUTION OF INDEFINITE AND CONFUSED IDEAS

The translation of an abstract idea or an image into a concrete form, making the intangible tangible, requires the most disciplined and rigorous kind of thinking. It demands clarification of half-realized images, impressions, intuitive feelings, and recollections. It requires that a person bring them into a perceivable form, which he can examine and evaluate for self-clarification as well as for shared communication.

You might hear someone say, "I have the most beautiful painting up here in my head." Possibly. But it is what happens between the image in his mind and the brush on the canvas that tests all the sensibilities. The artist himself does not know exactly what he will say visually or how it will look until it takes visible form. Then he must critique what he has done, deciding what to extend and what to exclude, making art a dialogué with his self as surely as it is a statement for others. To capture a vision and cast it in bronze is to attempt the impossible.

But then, that's the attraction. Artists, like scientists, are always trying to do what can't be done, trying to say what can't be said, breaking accepted limitations. The history of progress in any culture is written by these kinds of people.

Most of the time the artist is doing something he has not done before, making something he has not seen before—and he is doing it alone. He makes commitments to himself and he follows through. He develops trust in his own convictions. He is forced to, because there is no one to ask. He takes big chances and makes big mistakes in order to make big discoveries. The child, at his level, works in the same way. His discoveries are big to him and he is learning something about trusting his own judgment. Through the arts, we can give the child every chance to follow his own urges rather than follow a leader, so he can clarify and synthesize and be willing to make commitments. In this way, he forms habits of thinking and working that give him the foundation for becoming a sensitive adult.

Qualities strengthened: persistence
                            visualizing ability
                            independence
                            sensitivity
                            clarification
                            courage based on convictions

LEARNING THROUGH THE ARTS DEVELOPS THE ABILITY TO FUNCTION IN THE MIDST OF CHANGE

Art requires improvisation. So does living. Synthesizing facts and concepts into a new format implies change. Each time we accept a new idea or new way of proceeding into our thinking, we are forced to alter our present habits to accommodate it. Openness to new possibilities and experiences requires our continual adjustment of familiar ways of making and doing, and reevaluation of our values—we hold some and discard others. This is a growth process, one which is continuously changing.

Many people in our society find it hard to cope with change in their environment, their relationships, or themselves. One stumbling block is fear, of failure or of being different. These lend to fear of change, which stifles the free spirit. It is not possible to be innovative and safe at the same time. The arts make this very clear. As mentioned previously, we must take big chances and be willing to make big mistakes in order to make big discoveries, to make leaps beyond our usual capacities. Then we transcend ourselves. We are changed. That's the whole point. If we could help our students to understand that change in this sense is constructive rather than threatening, that it is a requirement of growth and progress, they might have less anxiety in their future lives. From this point of view, dealing with change becomes a natural and acceptable function of daily experience.

Qualities strengthened: openness
                                  flexibility
                                  tolerance for ambiguity
                                  self-renewal

Finally, **LEARNING THROUGH THE ARTS BUILDS SELF-DISCIPLINE** because it strengthens the ability to:

    appreciate the value of experiencing, rather than passive speculating, because the arts require making and doing;
    detect relationships and recognize metaphors because the arts develop creative thinking skills;
    concentrate on a single area of interest over a substantial period of time because the arts increase the ability to concentrate;
    trust one's own judgment because the arts foster the ability to make decisions;
    preserve in clarifying confused ideas and images because the arts require the resolution of indefinite and confused ideas;
    search for appropriate answers in the midst of frustration and flux because the arts value improvisation and the ability to function in the midst of change.

Self-discipline is a necessary ingredient of each of these abilities.

Papíer mâché sculpture by the author

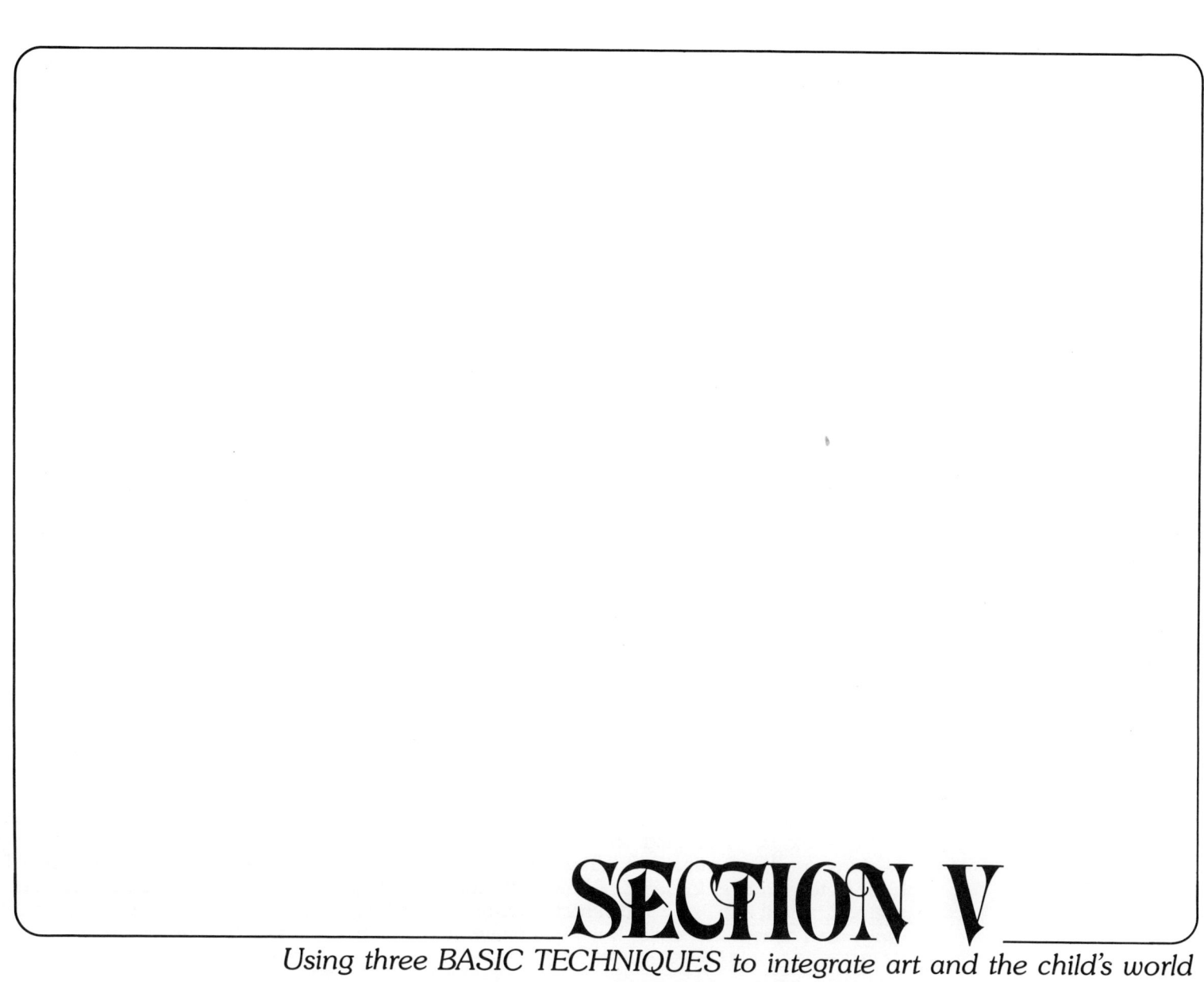

SECTION V
Using three BASIC TECHNIQUES to integrate art and the child's world

DRAWING

Learning to draw really means learning to see. Anyone can learn to express in line what he sees, as easily as he learns to read or speak. The secret is practice. Draw, draw, draw.

Why should a child spend time learning to draw, learning to think and communicate in a visual language? Because by drawing he rediscovers the world. He may never quite see what is there until he looks carefully enough to understand and draw it. Almost every activity in his day requires visual capabilities. He is surrounded with visual clues. His successful participation and decision-making depend on his ability to recognize the available clues and possibilities, before coming to conclusions. A good deal of student incompetence in the classroom can be traced to information, much of it visual, he has incompletely assimilated or overlooked entirely.

In drawing, the eye, heart, head, and hand must come together. It is the best kind of training for concentration whether the child is drawing something from his real world or from his imagination and memory. Given enough time, anyone can discover the basis principles of drawing by looking, thinking, and drawing often; but, since time is limited, guidance from the teacher is imperative. In the first through third grades the teacher usually calls attention to comparative sizes, placement, and perhaps texture. The child does not need technical suggestions or rules about how to draw things. Trial and error is far better process for learning than a rigid step-by-step method, and it allows for individual differences. Methodology can teach the child how to imitate and record nature—but that is not art. What he thinks about nature is what is important. Observing what he chooses to emphasize or ignore reveals a great deal about his perception of the subject, what he sees clearly, and what he has not clarified and thus cannot put into line. A sensitive teacher, with or without art training, can bring the child to focus and see through questioning and encouragement.

The teacher should stay with simple and familiar objects at first. If each child has an object in hand to draw, the teacher can ask specific questions about proportion and relationship of parts that the child can answer by observing and measuring the object. With both teacher and child looking at the same thing at the same time, consensus is easier. If a child is working from imagination, on the other hand, the teacher accepts the drawing as it comes because it is subjective, an inner vision, rather than objective.

If the child uses a real object, let it suggest the drawing implement if possible. For example, self-portrait is better done with pencil than crayon because the thick crayon line makes detail difficult. And although pen and ink allows clear detail, it can be frightening for the beginning artist because the line is irrevocable and he still needs to know he can move his lines if necessary. With confidence comes the courage for pen and ink. If the students are drawing furry live animals like rabbits or hamsters, motion rather than detail is important and with crayon or chalk they can draw quickly, using it broadside for wider, faster strokes.

A last reason for drawing. If it gives the student real pleasure, a fuller understanding of his world, and a sense of accomplishment, then the activity is of value. That's what art is about, too.

Start with Line Drawing. Children are well acquainted with a pencil so the tool is nonthreatening. Since they will see this as an identification game rather than a drawing lesson, they will likely relax, enjoy, and therefore do well. Move into Self-Portraits and Contour Drawings with its related activities, Organizing, which is basic to all visual work. It fits into an advanced first-, second- and third-grade curriculum. Outdoor Sketching and Drawing Nature can begin at second and third grade. Since classes vary widely this sequence may require reshuffling to better fit needs and abilities. Also, any one of the activities may be used individually if the class has already had some drawing practice.

Line Drawing

MATERIALS
- Newsprint paper
- Soft pencil or felt-tip pen

BOOKS
- Simpson, *Drawing: Seeing and Observation* (Van Nostrand Reinhold).
- Wachowiak and Ramsey, *Emphasis: ART*, Chapter VI (Crowell).
- Nicolaides, *The Natural Way to Draw* (Houghton Mifflin).
- Kampman, *Creating with Crayons* (Van Nostrand Reinhold).

INTERRELATING
Language arts—shape recognition and retention are basic requirements of reading skills. Drawing is excellent practice in visual discrimination and develops observation skills that, for instance, equip the child to readily distinguish d from b and q from p.

NEW VOCABULARY
- format
- similarity
- difference
- line drawing

PURPOSE

- To strengthen observation skills, eye-hand coordination, and tactile sensitivity
- To develop shape recognition and retention—a visual vocabulary
- To associate real objects with their symbols
- To make comparisons, experience ordering and synthesizing

PROCEDURE (K–3)

First experience

Distribute a paper bag containing one simple object (a comb, pencil, spoon) to each child in the class—a different object for each one if possible. (The children must not look inside.) They are to reach in, feel the object, then draw it on newsprint paper, still feeling it if they wish. When all have finished, have them take the objects out and compare them with the drawings. Talk of similarities and differences.

This learning game has anticipation, suspense, and resolution. Children thoroughly enjoy it and are willing to play again and again. Practicing two or three times a week over a period of several months develops and refines their tactile senses and eye-hand coordination. The game can be made suitable for any grade level by varying the complexity of the objects.

Second experience

This exercise is very good for developing visual retention. Space all the objects from the bag game on a table top so they are not touching. Ask the students to observe the collection carefully, then cover it with paper or an old sheet. They are to return to their newsprint and draw as many objects as they can recall. When they have finished, remove the sheet and name the shapes so each can check his drawing. Rearrange, add to, or subtract from the items and have them try it again. Watch visual retention skills grow over a period of weeks.

The first and second experience might be done with cardboard letters as well as objects.

Third experience

This is an extended practice in observing and ordering. Place a sheet of paper on the table top, and arrange three or four objects on it. This gives a clear impression of placement within a format (the size and shape of the paper). Define the word *format* for the students and use it often. Have them duplicate the relative placement of the objects as nearly as possible in their drawings. As they move around the table observing the layout, suggest they get an overall impression as well as noting specific placements. This exercise sharpens their awareness of position and relationship in context. As their perceptions grow, add to the objects on the table, or change the objects themselves each time. See how many they can recall and place, with additional practice.

Self-Portraits

MATERIALS
> soft pencil
> white paper
> mirror

PURPOSE
> Strengthen observation skills, of facial characteristics in particular
> Learn approximate proportion and placement of features and make comparisons
> Describe a three-dimensional subject with line alone

PROCEDURE (K-3)

Making self-portraits is an engaging class or small-group activity. Set up one or two mirrors in a quiet part of the room where students may do their portraits as a supplementary activity on an on-going basis. There is a fascination about the process and most children become genuinely involved after the preliminary ruffles and flourishes about looking at themselves. Even the most restless student will usually complete the portrait because he is so interested in the subject matter.

In kindergarten and first grade, just let the students draw on their own. By second or third grade, however, some visual facts about the proportions and placement of the features may be helpful. Have the whole class work with you in putting together a generalized diagram as a guide. Draw a large egg-oval on the chalkboard and strike a vertical line through the center from the top of the head to the tip of the chin.

You or a student may act as model. If you use a student, you will be free to help the class check proportions. From their seats, they pick up their pencils, extend their writing arms in front of them, elbows straight, sighting along the pencils to the model's face. Then, sliding their thumbs up and down the pencils as indicators:

1. Measure the distance from the top of the head to an imaginary horizontal line drawn through the eyes.
2. Measure the distance from the tip of the chin to the same line.
3. Compare the two measurements. They will find the eyes come close to the horizontal center of the head, much to everyone's consternation. They want to put them up next to the hair line. You draw this eye line on the chalkboard.
4. Measure the horizontal length of the eye and compare it with the distance between the eyes. It should be about the same. You mark the diagram.
5. Measure the length of the nose. Isn't it about the same as the distance from the end of the nose to the chin? You mark the diagram.
6. Strike a mark halfway between the nose mark and tip of the chin.
7. Measure the model and see if the mouth comes above, below, or on this line. Every person will vary a bit from the measurements—they are just reminders.
8. Compare the length of the nose with the height of the forehead and mark it.
9. Investigate the placement of the ears. Where does the top of the ear come in relation to the eye line? They should coincide.
10. Is the ear lobe almost on a line with the end of the nose?
11. Compare the width of the neck with the width of the face. You mark the diagram.
12. Suggest they treat the hair as a total shape. Draw its contour rather than putting in each hair individually.

This is the foundation on which they draw the individual face in detail. Remind them as often as necessary not to finish any feature until they have the face all blocked in. For some reason they love to put in highly detailed eyes and lashes right away, often to find the placement is wrong. Having spent much time with this careful rendering, they're not about to move the eyes for better or for worse. The portrait is never quite "right" —they know it and loose interest. From the blocking in to completion, the direction is their own. Colored pencils or pens, paint, pastels, or chalk may be used for subsequent portraits.

The students will enjoy these as a classroom exhibit. As a follow-up, have them draw each other, then compare the results of how they saw themselves with how others saw them.

Contour Drawing

MATERIALS
Newsprint or butcher paper
Soft pencil or felt-tip pen

BOOKS
Gaitskell and Hurwitz, *Children and Their Art,* Chapters III & VII.
Dimonstein, *Exploring the Arts with Children,* Part II, Concepts and Explorations (Macmillan).
Belvin, *Design Through Discovery* (Holt, Rinehart & Winston).
Emerson, *Design: A Creative Approach* (International Text Books).
Garrett, *Visual Design: A Problem Solving Approach* (Van Nostrand Reinhold).

INTERRELATING
Physical education—Body balance and physical balance have common roots
Math—basic concepts of balance, symmetry, and asymmetry in art have a counterpart in math

PURPOSE
Experiment with the arrangement of simple visual material to express an idea
Refine the thinking skills of ordering and sequencing through the use of line drawing
Explore principles of organization: balance, spacing, movement, and unity with variety
Learn the definition and some uses of contour drawing

NEW VOCABULARY

asymmetry   symmetry
contour   repetition
outline   design
balance   radial balance
movement

PROCEDURE

First experience (1–3)

Contour drawing means drawing only the outside edge of a thing—an outline. As an example, have each student put one hand, with fingers spread apart, on his paper and draw around it. Voilà! A contour drawing. Look at it together. By questioning, you can help them discover that this drawing doesn't show if the person is wearing rings, certainly not what kind, or where the knuckles and lines come, or whether the hands are clean or dirty. A contour drawing only talks about edges, but it can be very useful. It speaks of shape, size, and sometimes spacing, as, for instance, between the fingers. Rembrandt made telling contour drawings. So do a number of contemporary cartoonists and commercial designers.

Second experience (1–4)

Have each student gather three to five objects between the size of an eraser and a pair of scissors. They can probably find them in their desks; or, several days before this exercise, ask them to bring in some small objects like juice cans, bottle tops, shells. To reinforce the concept of contour, the students will draw around these objects repeatedly, to create a design or pattern.

This provides a perfect opportunity to talk about and arrange shapes to convey a visual idea, just as every artist does. With organization, an artist attempts to bring disparate units together to create a functioning, satisfying whole, the way a teacher takes a group of heterogeneous individuals in September and organizes them into a productive, functioning classroom.

Some of the principles of organization in art are balance, unity with variety, movement, spacing. Although the principles overlap in actual practice and cannot be separated, it is less confusing for the student if one is emphasized at a time and their relatedness unfolds naturally.

Movement (2–4)

It is most fun to use wrapping paper or butcher paper so the kids can draw long lines of shapes moving across the paper in a variety of ways. They pick up on their own movements. Ask that they have their shape make a 100-yard dash from one edge to the other. This will tend to be a straight fast line.

Below the dash line, have them show how their shape would move on its way to school if it had lots of time and interesting things to examine. It should meander.

Compare the two. If the students showed these two lines to a stranger could his eye follow the trail drawn and understand how the shapes moved? Which was fast and which was slow? Yes, he could. Next have each think

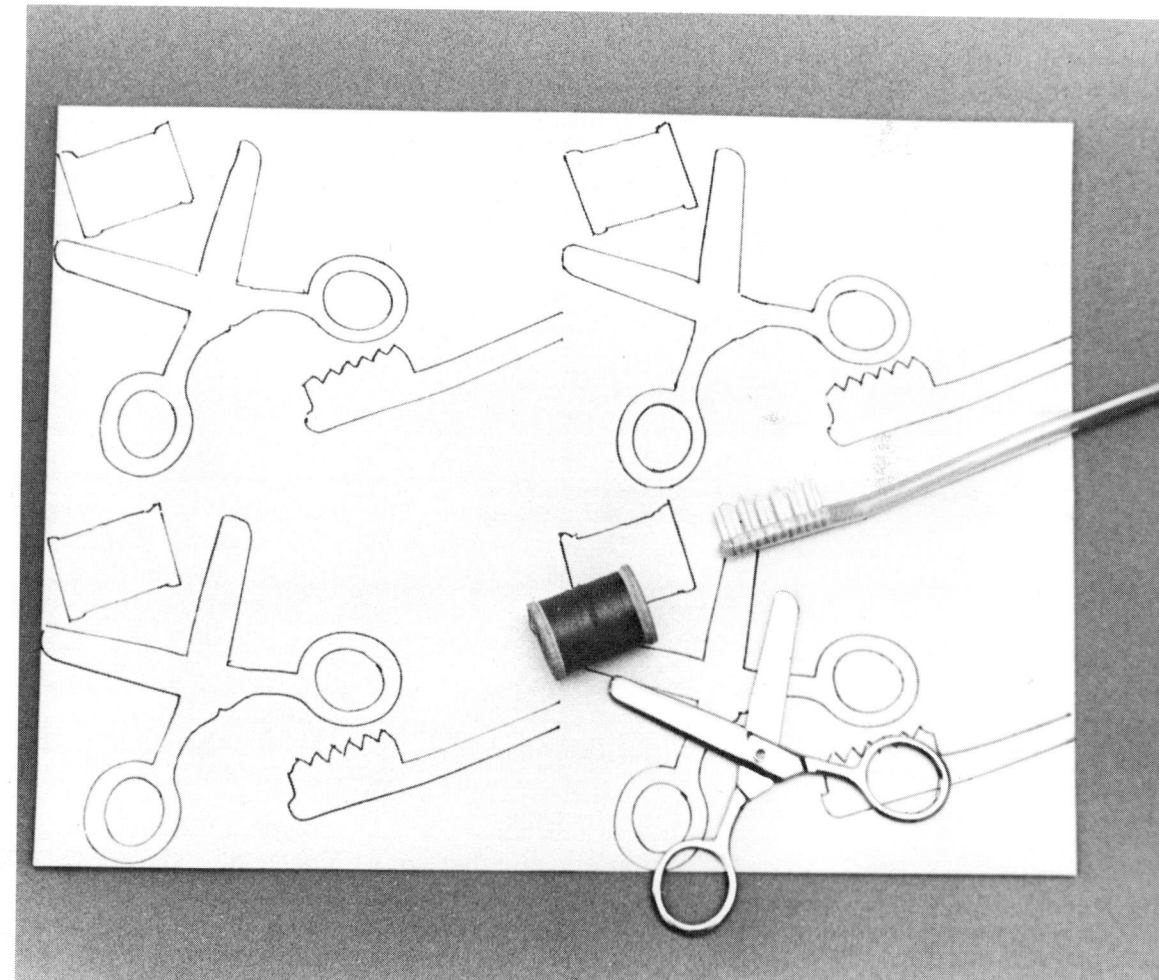

of a movement for his shape, then share his drawing with the class. See if they can guess what he had in mind.

Printing Shapes (1–3)

Students may feel a need, when working with movement, to manipulate shapes more quickly for a flow of action. Round up some sink stoppers and stamp pads or make some with tempera paint (see page 39 for instructions) and let them stamp a trail with the sink stopper. Incidentally, they also make contour circles. Here the importance of the contour yields to the more important idea that shapes arranged in certain ways give clear messages.

PRINCIPLES OF ORGANIZATION
presented as activities

Balance (1–3)

Symmetrical balance is the easiest for children to understand, recognize, and reproduce. Have some of them fold a half piece of construction or ditto paper in half, vertically, and the remaining group fold it in half, horizontally. Open the sheet and draw some shapes and lines (no scribbling) with heavy contour pencil on one side of the fold. Fold to close with the drawing inside the top half. Cover the outside (top) with enough side-of-the-pencil rubbings to transfer the drawing to the opposite side. Open. This is a straight one-to-one correspondence, an easily seen mirror image. With your questions and their reactions, you can show that the drawings are even orderly and that simple repetition yields a design of sorts.

Asymmetrical balance is another kind of arrangement. Children can physically feel the difference between asymmetrical and symmetrical balance by standing up, putting all their weight on one leg, bending the other one at the knee, and holding this position as long as they can. Then, have them place both feet on the ground spaced slightly apart with weight distributed equally. Heads up and hands clasped behind their back makes for a perfectly symmetrical stance. It is possible to balance in both positions. Ask them which was easier (the second). The one-foot stand is harder to control. So, in art, asymmetry is "harder to control" because it is a more sophisticated concept and is best dealt with after the child has a grip on a few more basics.

A third type of balance is radial. Have them mark off a small center circle at the center of their papers. Distribute the shapes out from that center like the spokes of a wheel, in the form of a bull's-eye or in ways they create, always working in a circular movement. When these are hung up for display, notice how the eye keeps searching out the center of the designs.

Spacing and Unity with Variety (2–5)

Have them fold the paper in half horizontally, then in half vertically, so when opened it has four equal boxes. Pick one shape and draw around it the same way in the same spot in each rectangle. Ask them if this repetition would tend to get boring after five or six pages. How could they vary it? Choose another shape of a different size, and draw it next to or over part of the first shape, in all four boxes. Try a third shape if needed. A pattern occurs, giving a kind of unity with variety. This makes it possible for us to look at two or three different kinds of objects at one time because of the structure and order in which they occur.

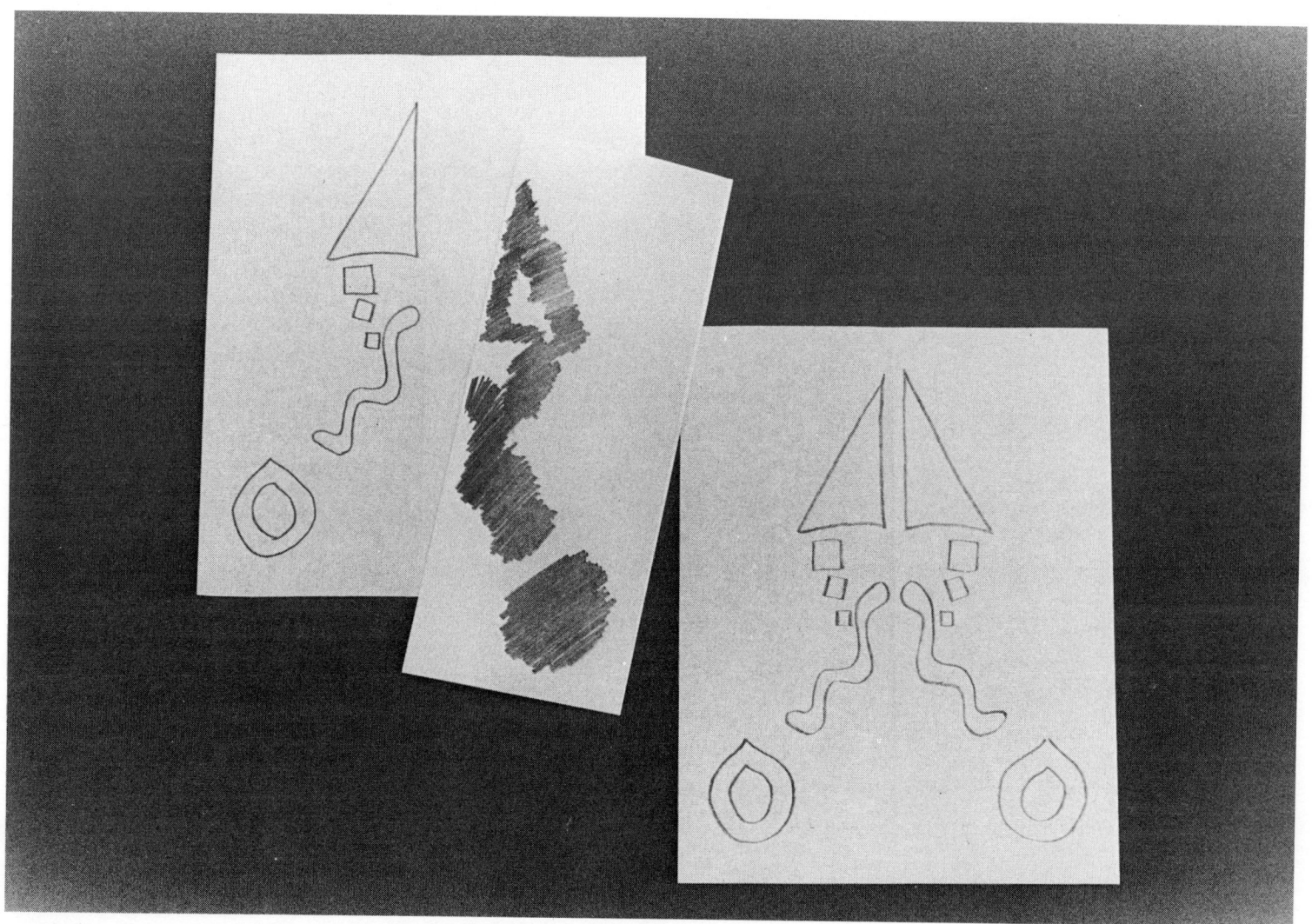

Outdoor Sketching

MATERIALS
Newsprint or drawing paper
Soft pencil

BOOKS
Allison, *The Reason for Seasons* (Little, Brown).
Mugnaini, *The Hidden Elements of Drawing* (Van Nostrand Reinhold).

INTERRELATING
The "real" world and the student's school world come together in a natural and productive way

PURPOSE
Develop shape recognition and retention
Strengthen concept of spatial relationships
Explore relative size relationships
Order and arrange visual information
Broaden the child's working knowledge through careful observation of surroundings

VOCABULARY (review)
format
outline
contour

PROCEDURE (3–4)

Outdoor sketching for the third- and fourth-grade child is almost a lost art. This is unfortunate because it is an exciting way to awaken the child to numerous, as yet unnoticed things in his surroundings. Drawings can be done in the school yard, the playground, the city park—any location where each child can have a comfortable spot and an uninterrupted view. If the children seem overwhelmed at first by so much detail, remind them that they are just to draw the contours of the objects. If this proves to be a valuable activity, you can have them add detail later, after several of these drawings.

Some children are helped by using a "window," a 3″ × 5″ card with a window cut out the approximate shape of the paper. The student holds it at arm's length, elbows straight, and moves it across the landscape until he finds a view he likes or one on which you have all agreed. This frame separates his vista from its surroundings and tells him what to include in his drawing. If he includes some other things, that's all right too. It is mainly a device for getting him started. Some children need a lot of encouragement to put any kind of view down on paper.

The teacher without much formal art training should not hesitate to try this activity, for his role is to awaken the student's vision to what is there. Call attention to size relationships between bushes and trees, windows and doors, and the spaces between these shapes. This aids the child in pinpointing a few locations on his paper. Talk about the objects in terms of basic shapes. This is like a circle, or that is like a square, or a combination of them. The quality of the drawings will improve amazingly after several of these sessions. So will the student's understanding of "how things are." This contour drawing can later be colored, collaged, or used as a component for a mural or a more detailed study.

Drawing Nature

MATERIALS
    Newsprint or drawing paper
    Soft pencil or felt-tip pen
    Crayons, oil pastel, or watercolor

BOOKS
    Hogarth, *Creative Pencil Drawing* (Watson Guptill).

PURPOSE
    Discover color, form, and size relationships in everyday surroundings
    Identify and select pertinent information for describing a growth process
    Strengthen and clarify visually perceived information

NEW VOCABULARY
    monocotyledon
    dicotyledon

INTERRELATING
    Science—observing a growth process through visual clues, patterns, and questioning techniques clarifies the information necessary for the student's translation of it into drawing and, at the same time, reinforces his understanding of the process

PROCEDURE

First experience (2−3)

Combining a science or environmental activity with art can facilitate learning in both areas. Sometime during the year when you have a plant growing project, incorporate drawing into the study. Since careful observation is required for drawing, examining the stages of plant development takes on a practical purpose and can strengthen children's awareness of the growth process.

Suppose you choose to draw a sweet potato, beginning to leaf out, which the class has had in water. Again, using simple contour drawing, begin by looking at the plant and asking some questions. Both visual and verbal information will surface through directed conversation with the students while they are drawing. This feeds them immediately usable data and has a relaxing effect—they will produce a freer flow of line. Had they noticed that the older leaves are larger than the new baby ones? Which are closer to the potato? Does it shoot out a leaf at equal intervals or in clusters along the stem? We've talked about spacing for design and pattern—this plant seems to know a good deal about both. Why are the leaves so spaced and not bunched together? Would it have something to do with every leaf needing light for growth? If children are using color, ask them which leaves are dark green and which are lighter, more yellow, green and why. This kind of questioning will force them to look more closely and thus strengthen their awareness of the growth process.

Second experience (2−3)

A fresh approach to germinating seeds involves keeping a daily journal recording growth by having the children draw the progress. This requires them to examine the most minute changes, which is excellent visual training. Using bean and pea seeds, which are both dicotyledon, and popcorn, which is monocotyledon, sets up basic similarities and differences. As you discuss the appearance of the seeds and what their needs for growing will be, draw pictures of all three for future reference.

Plant the seeds in separate labeled containers, place them in the sun, and keep them moist. At the same time, put one or two of each kind of seed halfway down a glass jar, holding them in place against the glass with a rolled paper towel, which will be kept moist. Place the jar in a dark place. Students can observe this germination process through the glass. Keep a drawing record of both processes over a period of seven to ten days after some sprouting begins to show. Comparisons can easily be made. When finished and placed in a row, the two sets of drawings become clear examples of the idea of sequence and growth.

PAINTING

To paint is to be free. Free to choose, to paint whatever colors in whatever way for whatever reason. A free act of self-expression. Paint should always be available for the kindergarten and first-grade child. It is splendid stuff of color and flow. Either brush or finger painting should hold an important position in the kindergarten curriculum and beyond.

Opaque dry or liquid tempera is suitable and available in schools. Finger painting is the most basic technique, and the most fun—a good place to start for children in the manipulative stage. Tempera can be mixed with liquid or cornstarch, wheat paste or buttermilk, and spooned onto damp butcher paper or shelf paper. It is smart to cover work surfaces with newspaper and have each student wear an apron. Students should not have to worry about spattering paint—it's inhibiting.

Each begins in his own way; some with a finger, cautiously working up to the hand; some jump in with both hands, an arm, and a leg. They quickly finish the painting, wipe it out, and begin again. This fits the urge of the kindergarten—first-grader to get images on paper as fast as they come to thought. After working with one color for a while, the child can add a second in dry or liquid form; he has the joy of discovering a third color as the first two mix. Allowing a few children to paint at one time allows for easy control and clean-up. This is a messy activity.

Easel painting or painting on the floor begins with one color. By adding one color each week or after each series of four or five sessions, the child gets a gradual introduction to mixing color and thinking in hues. A regular painting period will assure his ability to name and manipulate seven or eight colors by the end of the year.

Children tend to be quite spontaneous with their painting in the beginning. They just need materials and elbow room. When the pace begins to slow or interest begins to wane, the three activities outlined can reawaken interest. Tile Painting is fine for kindergarten through third grade. Working with new materials is stimulating; older children enjoy seeing their painting transformed into a permanent, fired decoration on tile, an added dimension. Painting Poems, also for kindergarten through third grade, invites the students to respond to the unexpected and to word pictures structured into the poem. Found Object Painting for second and third grade leaves two-dimensional painting for a fling at painting familiar objects and making them first strange, then new.

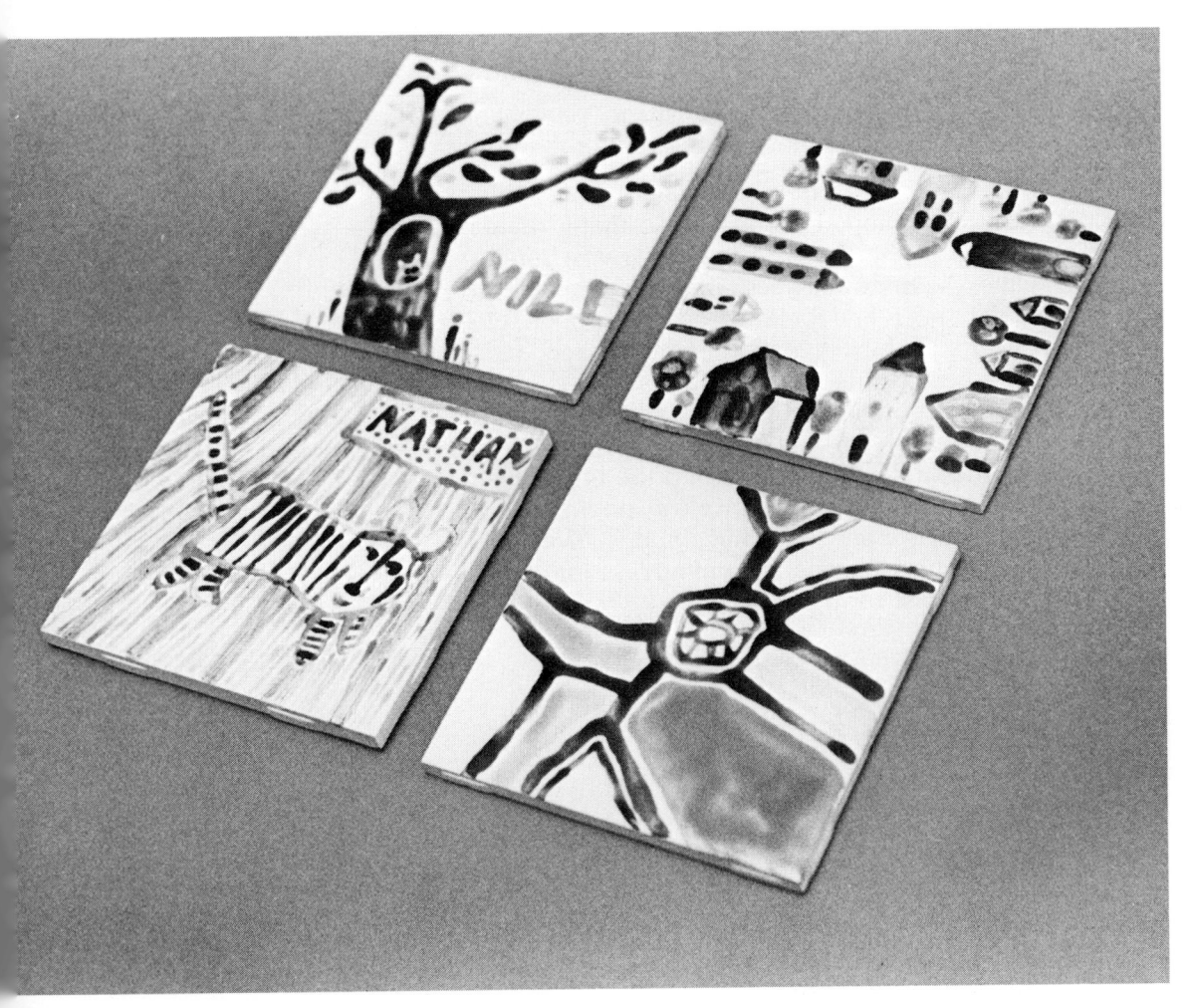

MATERIALS

Titles 4" × 4" or larger white glazed commercial titles
Glazes—primary colors and black
Brushes—#7, #5, or #6 if available
Lead pencil

BOOKS

McIlvain, *Art for the Primary Grades* (Putman).
Mattil, *Meaning in Crafts* (Prentice-Hall).

PURPOSE

Develop ability to cooperate and work in a group
Practice arranging shapes and colors in a format —designing

NEW VOCABULARY

title
glaze
primary colors

PROCEDURE (K-3)

Making a gift for someone is as exciting to a child as the anticipation of giving it. Tile painting is a creative experience, and the product is both original and attractive. By following a few suggestions, every child can be successful. The glossy, colorful finshed tiles will delight the class.

The designs on the 4" × 4" tiles may be complicated or simple, according to each child's preference.

Success usually depends on how well he can manipulate a brush. But then, the kindergarten child who just writes his first name with its confused capital and lower-case letters and backward N's creates an irresistible contemporary family heirloom.

Making tile from clay is tricky and difficult for children. Tiles must be of uniform thickness and have some semblance of right-angle corners. In addition, they are difficult to fire without warping. Buying plain, white glazed tiles from a local tile supplier is a perfect solution. The student paints directly on the glazed surface with liquid colored glaze, whose consistency is so similar to paint that application is easy.

Each child should write his name on the tile back with a lead pencil. Crayon or anything greasy will disappear during firing.

Buy the primary colors and black, in hi-gloss glaze. These are available at any ceramic or hobby shop. Use a standard #5 or #6 paint brush. The smaller brushes control the amount of glaze put on the tile and also make lines easier to draw. The glaze should be thick enough so the brush marks do not allow the white tile to show through.

A basic problem is keeping the glaze colors pure. Children will become excited and put the blue brush into the yellow glaze without thinking, even if they have been cautioned not to mix the colors. Within minutes the yellow becomes green. To avoid this, put yellow glaze and a number of brushes at one table, the blue at a second, and so on. However, this form of control is discouraging for some children who work more freely with access to all colors at one time. If an aide is available to sit at the table with the various glaze colors, and if several brushes are provided for each color so no one has to wait, everything should move smoothly. Brushes can be washed in clear water, wiped on a cloth, and reused immediately. If water is left in the brush it will dilute the glaze to a pastel.

A few children will find the whole experience so appealing they may attempt to paint the edges and back of the tile. This will glue the tile to the kiln shelf when fired and is to be avoided. The top side only is paintable. Don't worry if they puddle the glaze here and there on the tile—it will fire beautifully. After the painting is finished put the tile out of reach and allow it to dry. In half an hour or so it can be fired. Tiles can be reclaimed before firing by rinsing the glaze off and drying the surface. They are then ready to be painted again.

Watch for the child who layers on all colors of glaze then scrubs around in them until the tile is mud colored. Often he needs a clearer idea of something to paint. A good preliminary to this whole activity is a paint-on-paper session. If this is motivated by a story, a nature walk, or a field trip, he wll have something fresh in mind to put in the painting, then on the tile.

It will be easy to get volunteers to do an extra tile. These can become a permanent display in your room; glue them on strips of wood with epoxy and mount them over the door frame and down the side for 24 inches or so as a colorful, original frame.

Painting Poems

MATERIALS
  Tempera
  Brushes
  Paper

BOOKS
  Arbutknot, *Children and Books* (Scott, Foresman).
  Arbutknot, *Time for Poetry* (Scott, Foresman).
  Chukovsky, *From Two to Five* (University of California Press).
  de Regniers, *Poems Children Will Sit Still For* (Scholastic Book Serivces).
  Livingston, *Wide Awake* (Harcourt, Brace and World).
  Kampman, *The Children's Book of Painting* (Van Nostrand Reinhold).
  Scott, *Finger Painting* (Batsford).

INTERRELATING
  Language arts—through poetry and vocabulary extension

PURPOSE
  Experience sequencing in a new process
  Strengthen decision-making skills
  Select appropriate alternatives in designing
  Develop recall and visual memory
  Experiment with size relationships, textures, and color

NEW VOCABULARY
  location   solid color
  texture   proportion
  fantastic   concrete poetry

PROCEDURE (1-3)

Painting comes naturally to young children. Often by the first or second grade, however, the time allotted for this important activity is eroded by more academic pursuits. When the child does have a chance to paint, he finds his facility is slipping away through lack of practice. Self-consciousness sets in and motivation drops. His alternative is to continuously repeat his last successful painting.

One way to approach this problem is to give a painting assignment with a few surprises. Irresistible surprises are best. Try writing the directions in free verse:

Bright sun
Blue sky
Two clouds
One tree, another taller, only one green
Three birds in branches
One flying North
You are in the picture, under one tree
With a favorite friend.

When the students are ready to paint, put only the first line on the chalkboard. Wait until each has his bright sun finished before writing the second line. Continuing this line-by-line method will coax them to make frequent decisions, some accommodating to space, in short, to deal with a new process that requires thought. They will produce, at the very least, a fresh composition. No student can preconceive the final picture. The process forces evolution.

Poems can be composed to lead the students into and through a series of problem-solving adventures, requiring them to invent new images and fresh combinations. Take another look at the poem and the explanation of its form and sequence:

Bright sun Every child draws suns and this allows each to start with something he knows well.
Blue sky This is also easy.
Two clouds A little thought is required as to location, size, color, and shape; also whether to use line or solid color.
One tree, another taller, only one green
   They must consider location, size relationship, colors, line, shape, texture. Will they stand side by side? If a tree isn't green, what color is it?
Three birds in branches
   Again, they choose location, size, proportion, color, line, shape, and texture.
One flying North
   Where's North? Where the artist says it is!
You are in the picture, under one tree
   What are you wearing? How do you look?
With a favorite friend.
   Who's a favorite friend? His dog? John? A bird? A snake? A book?

Real, imagined, recalled, or prophetic encounters can be captured, visualized, and shared in this way.

From such beginnings, children can ease into poetry quite naturally. Concrete poetry or the poem as picture is a delightful pursuit for advanced second- and third-graders. It requires them to think on two levels at one time, visual and verbal. For example, have the class think up and write a number of words to describe "tree." Suppose they suggest tall green, leafy, branching, etc. This is good for both vocabulary extension and spelling. They can use these words to form their tree, using crayons or felt-tip pens on newsprint. For some, it may be easier to draw a tree first then fit in letters that spell the words. After the first try, share some of the class examples. The second ones will come easier.

Painting Found Objects

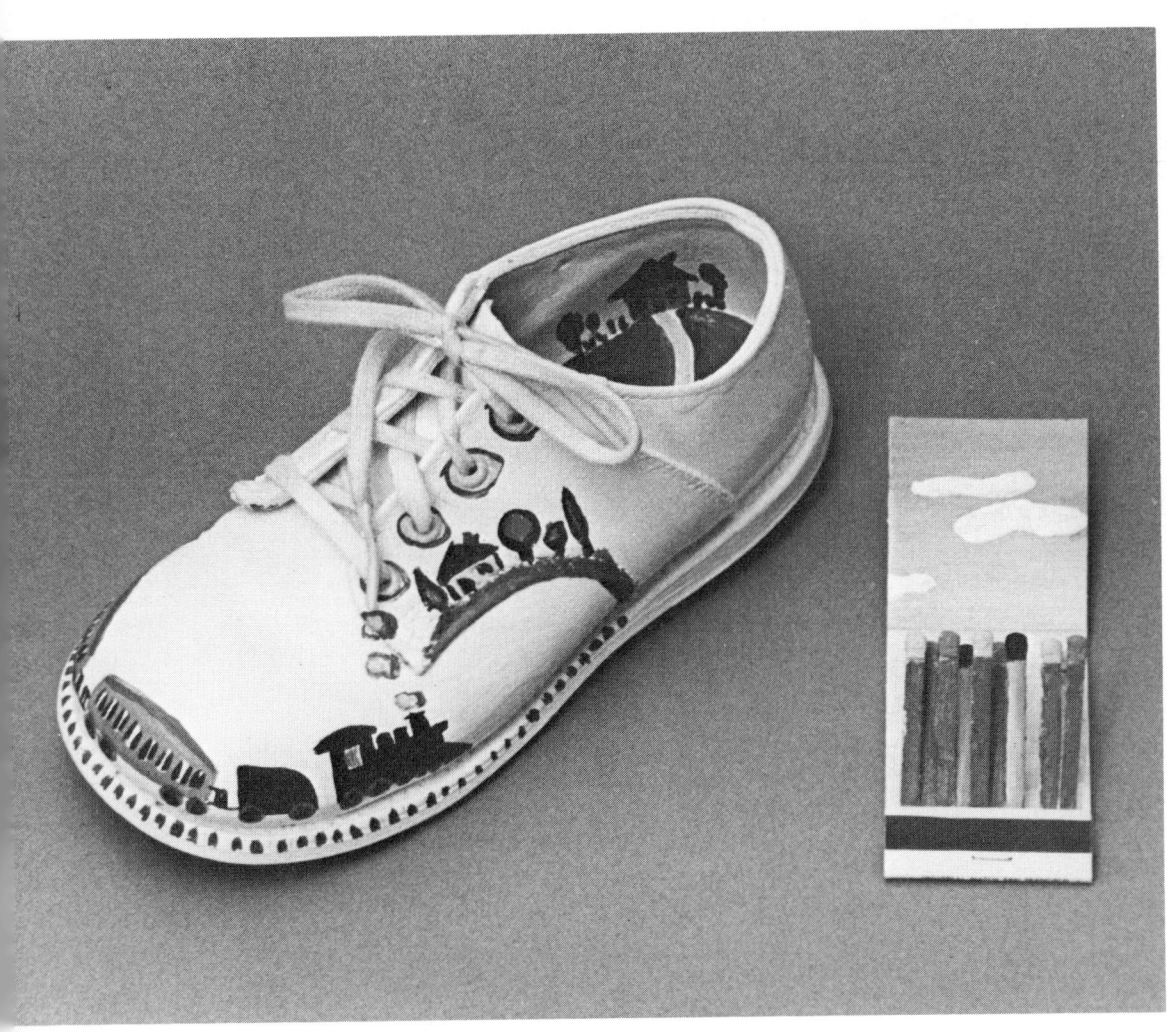

MATERIALS
    Collection of objects
    Latex paint (white or off-white)
    Tempera
    Brushes
    Butcher paper

BOOKS
    Laliberte and Mogelon, *Collage Montage Assemblage* (Van Nostrand Reinhold).
    Making It Strange (Booklets—A New Design for Creative Thinking and Writing) (Harper & Row)
    Siks, *Drama with Children* (Harper & Row)
    Siks, *Creative Dramatics* (Harper & Row)
    Mattil, *Meaning in Crafts* (Prentice-Hall)

INTERRELATING
    Social studies—folk art of other cultures: Mexican, Canadian, Indian, Eskimo, and American

PURPOSE
    Develop capacity to improvise and invent
    Encourage imagination
    Heighten awareness through visual and tactile experiences
    Design and paint on a three-dimensional surface

NEW VOCABULARY
    three-dimensional   fantasy
    shape   latex
    novel

PROCEDURE (1–3)

Painting on a three-dimensional surface brings a new excitement to the child who has only painted on paper or is reticent about painting in any form.

Painting on paper in kindergarten to third grade tells us about an object or experience from one point of view. It has immediate impact. All parts can be seen at one time and all shapes are perceived as flat. In painting on a three-dimensional object, say an old shoe, garden glove, or wishbone, children must consider all sides. They can transform a recognizable shape into something strange, something new. This kind of practice in improvising and inventing frees the imagination and encourages the child to see in fresh ways.

Try this activity with your class. A fanciful collection of objects is one key to success. Make a class game of bringing in contributions. Ask the students to bring in "shapes" that would take two hands to hold (too-small shapes are difficult and frustrating to paint). The word "shape" seems less limiting than "object." We tend to think of an object as some completed thing, whereas a shape might be half an object or a natural formation. Set up a table in the corner of the room for contributions. Put an old umbrella or hat on the table for openers.

Inspect and discuss the donations every day to build enthusiasm for the search. When examining each, turn it upside down to see it out of context. This helps the students develop an eye for a novel shape. They will also get an idea of the importance of shape as an element of an object's identity. You might even want to use some of the things for props in improvisational drama.

There are numerous ways of approaching the actual painting:

1 Paint the object with colors in pattern, or on the edges, as floating shapes, as line drawings, or as a combination of all these.
2 Paint the whole object in a patchwork of colors and proceed from there.
3 Show examples of Mexican, Eskimo, Indian, and/or American folk art. These cultures often applied designs and colors to functional three-dimensional pieces.
4 How would these shapes look if they all came to life?

If they had human characteristics—eyes and mouth, nose and ears? Ask the students what they envision. As an extension of this paint-on, have some of the children place the completed shape in the middle of a piece of butcher paper and describe on it, with paint and crayons, where it lives, where it sleeps, what it eats, or its favorite game. This invites fantasy.

Next, the students can tell about their painted shapes to an aide who will put these thoughts in written form. These can be read, instead of a book, at story time.

A note about the practical application of paint to shape; tempera will not stick to some surfaces successfully. Most schools have tempera, and if it must be used, a good mixture can be made with powdered tempera and

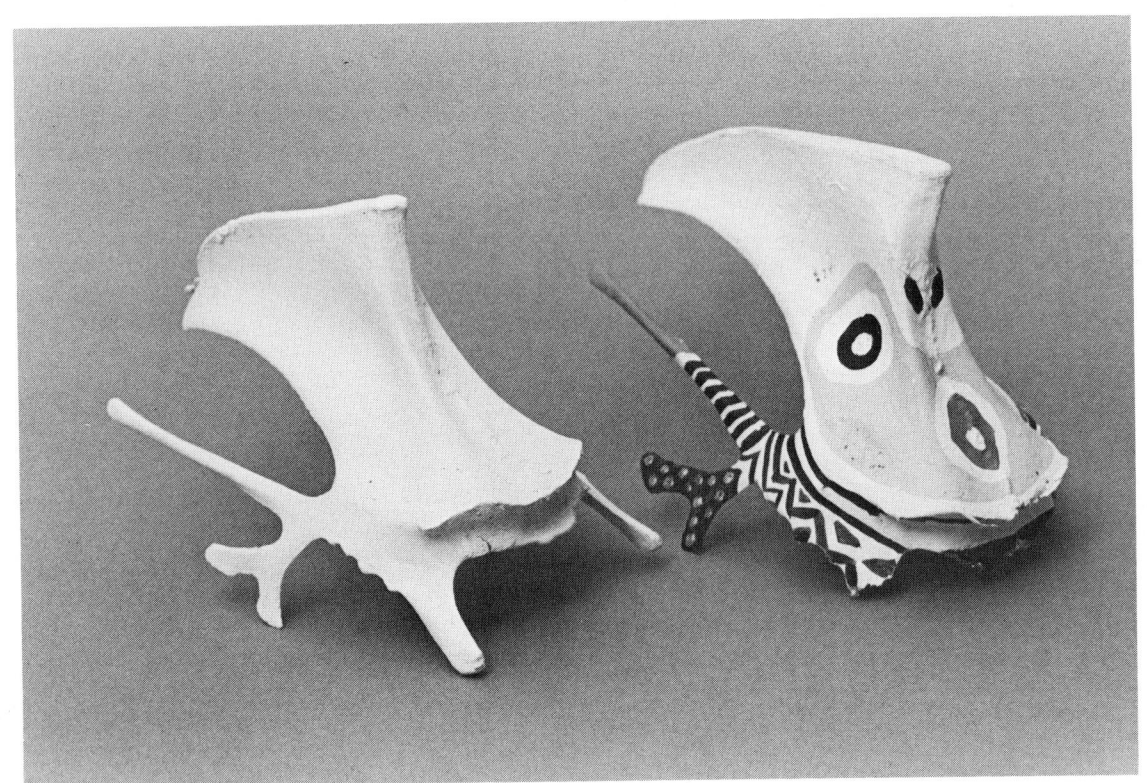

latex house paint. It is water soluble and is easily cleaned up. Liquid tempera can also be used. Send a letter home to parents asking for latex paint; two or three used half-gallons are usually sitting in parents' garages just waiting for such a cause. Mix the tempera into small amounts of paint for each child, being careful not to exceed one part tempera to two parts latex or the covering qualities will be impaired.

You can also start the project by allowing each child to completely paint his shape with white or off-white latex. This obliterates descriptive detail and makes the shape itself easier to see, thus helping the child decide where and how to place the colors.

CLAY

Clay may be the single most provocative art material for young children. It is tactile and responsive. It can be pounded, pinched, poked, and prodded, relieving anxieties and tensions. In fact, the energetic child can push it around endlessly without fear of damaging it, except that it may dry out. So, just add water and continue.

Allowing time for the child to develop a playful acquaintance with clay dissipates the pounding and pinching urge and replaces it with the desire to proceed more purposefully. Five or ten minutes is time well spent at the beginning of a clay activity. It awakens the impulse to model, to make, to feel and do.

An occasional child will not want to work with clay for fear of getting clothes or hands dirty. Slip a workshirt-smock on him. If this does not allay the fears, the thought of his hands in "mud" may be the problem. Have him do something else and the enthusiasm of the other children may convert him. If not, forcing compliance will serve no useful purpose.

Several suggestions about working with clay can make it easier for all. A 25-pound "plug" of coarse potter's clay is ideal. Coarse clay will take very rough treatment. It fires at cone .06. When not in use, firing clay must be kept in plastic bags, tightly closed, with a couple of wet sponges for moisture. Plan enough time so all the clay pieces can be completed in one sitting. Otherwise be prepared to cover each with a wet cloth and a plastic bag so it will be workable the second day. Be sure no foreign object like hairpins or toothpicks get into the clay—they will cause explosions in the kiln. Work on scrap plastic or oilcloth if the desk must be covered. Each child should have access to a plastic spray bottle of water. These control the amount of water a child uses and are preferable to pans of water. Children have a tendency to get the clay too wet; it should be just moist enough to be pliable.

If the clay dries out it can be reclaimed. Put it in a bucket with water equal to one-third its volume. In a couple of days it can be kneaded and used again. Sometimes bubbles appear in the fresh clay body. The potter kneads these out because they can cause explosions in the kiln, but with young children, clay naturally gets such a workout that the problem does not arise. However, using coarse clay is added insurance.

Provide enough clay for each child—about the size of a large grapefruit. Rotate small groups through a clay experience rather than giving each a bare handful. A plug will serve about fifteen children.

Teaching clay terminology through Clay Pantomime is a good way to start with beginners, especially kindergarten children. Then move naturally into experimentation, in Construction and Impressions. The Clay Creature, Group Structures, and Clay and Seeds activities are designed for second- and third-graders. However, some first-graders can handle these quite well.

Pantomime

MATERIALS
    Clay
    Imagination

BOOKS
    Howard, *Pantomime, Charades and Skits* (Sterline).

PURPOSE
    Learn basics of clay manipulation through pantomime
    Interpret "clay vocabulary" through mime
    Increase awareness of three-dimensional shape

NEW VOCABULARY

kneading	smoothing
rolling	squeezing
pantomime	scoring
pinching	

PROCEDURE (K–2)

For children who have not worked with clay before, the introductory session should emphasize process so they will sense that getting to know clay rather than making something is the objective.

The various terms used in clay manipulation—kneading, pinching, punching, squeezing, twisting, rolling, smoothing, and scoring—can be introduced through pantomime. Understanding them through action rather than verbal explanation alone is easier for children.

Give everyone an imaginary ball of clay large enough to require two hands to hold it. FEEL THE WEIGHT? Since "squeezing" is a word most children are familiar with, start there. TAKE THAT BALL AND SQUEEEEEEEEEEEZE IT. AGAIN. AND AGAIN. Pantomime one of the clay terms at a time until they are familiar to the children, then string several together. Work through sequences, now punching clay, then pinching it, then squeezing it again. Change context occasionally by asking how these actions would change with a lump of clay as large as a beach ball (small as a marble, covered with syrup).

The term *scoring* is very important for children to know and remember. When two pieces of clay are joined, the surfaces must be roughed up and moistened so the bond will hold. If this is not done, the pieces will come apart as they dry. Very disappointing. The teacher can demonstrate as he describes the process. In pantomime, separate the clay in two pieces. Rough up the area on each where it is to join the other. Use an imaginary fork and make furrows just deep enough to hold a bit of water, which you sprinkle on next. Then push one piece into the other and smooth out the surfaces. This is quite a bit for the class to remember but if they pantomime it several times, that will help set the sequence.

Pass out clay immediately after the pantomime session because they will all be ready. The larger the ball the better. Because clay is such a seductive material, students become entranced by its plastic qualities and are often so absorbed moving it around that they lose contact with instruction for a while. That's fine. Because of the pantomime practice they will be able to approach the real thing with several ideas about what to do.

Kindergarten children should not necessarily make something the first time. After five or ten minutes of free play, have them roll the clay into balls and collect them before they tire of manipulating it. Tell them they will work with clay the next day.

Constructions and Impressions

MATERIALS
    Clay
    Nylon fishing line (10 lb. test) from the local hardware
    Dowel rod, ⅛" diameter cut in 2" lengths
    Rolling pin
    Gadgets
    Tempera
    Glaze (optional)
    Tongue depressers, old pencils, forks, and spoons

BOOKS
    Mendoza, *A Wart Snake in a Fig Tree* (Dial).
    Lobel, *The Ice Cream Coot and Other Rare Birds* (Parents).
    de Paola, *The Tyrannosaurus Game* (Holiday House).
    Carle, *One Two Three to the Zoo* (Collins & World).
    Tallon, *Zoophabets* (Bobbs-Merrill).
    Dunning, *Reflections on a Gift of Watermelon Pickle* (poetry) (Lothrop).

INTERRELATING
    Language arts—using a story to motivate clay impressions of animals, birds, or almost anything

PURPOSE
    Explore capabilities of clay as a material
    Translate imaginative images into visual form
    Organize shapes through a construction process
    Develop skills, procedures, and techniques associated with working in clay
    Make concrete forms from verbal descriptions

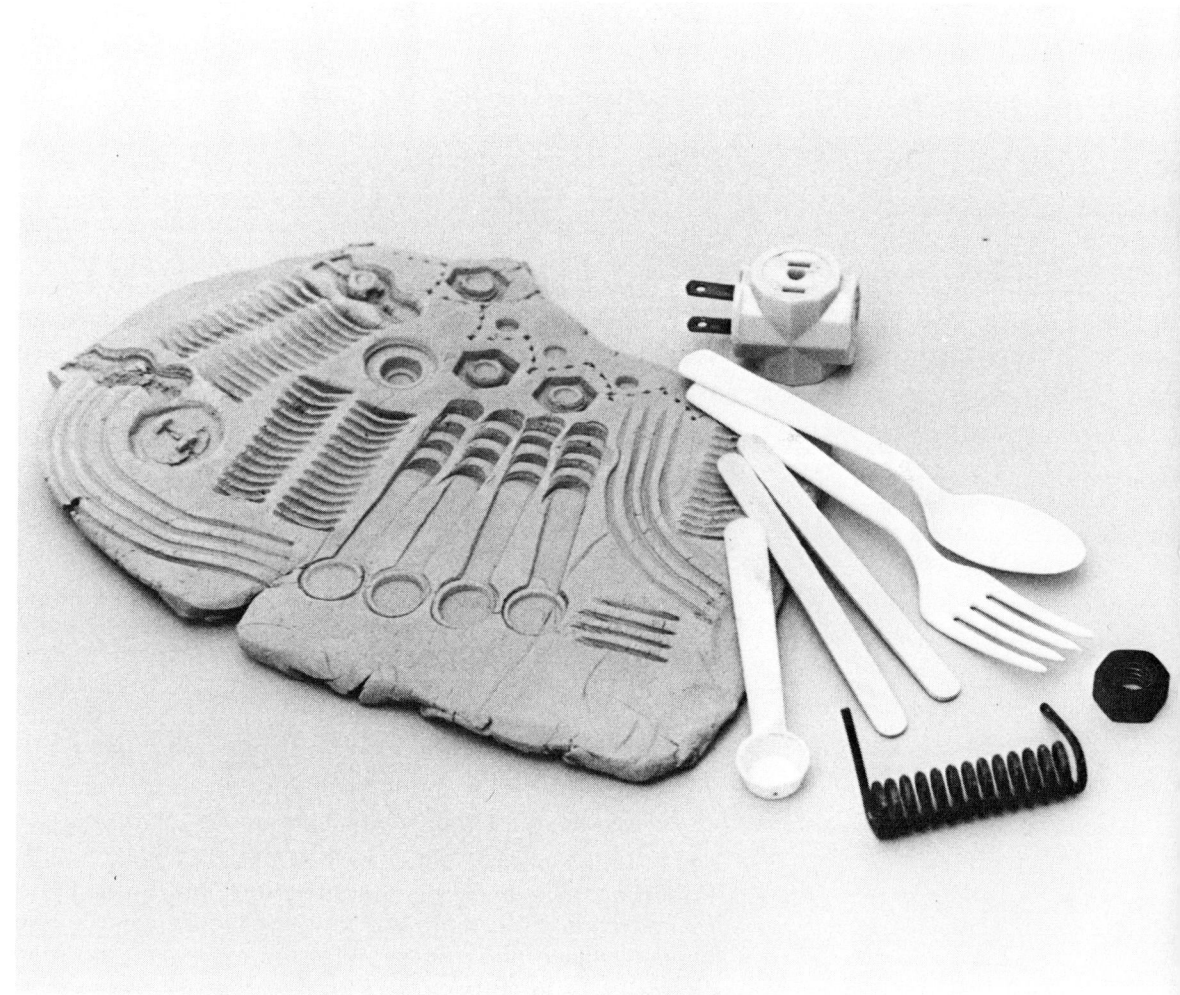

NEW VOCABULARY

slice	layer
stack	strip
slab	pile

PROCEDURE (1-3)

Clay is a building material and children need to know its capabilities. Given enough time they will discover these on their own; unfortunately, time is usually short. This simple series of explorations will introduce some basics in an unobtrusive way. They can spin these off in all directions.

Nylon fishing line is cheap and easy to manipulate. A piece 12" long with a spool tied on either end provides a perfect cutting edge for clay. As easily as cutting butter with a hot wire, each child can cut clay with this common tool to produce endless slabs, strips, and shapes we would never consciously think of. If spools are not available show them how to wrap an end around each hand then pull the line through the clay (use an 18" piece). How high can they pile their shapes before they topple over? Easy does it. Have a contest. This teaches patience, care in construction, the effect of weight, and some advantages and limitations of the material.

Show them how to make round balls by rolling small lumps of clay between the palms of both hands. Punch a dowel rod (⅛" diameter) through the ball and make beads. Fire them and let the children wear a clay bead necklace. (Toothpick holes are too small and may close during firing.)

Show them how to make long snakey coils and flat slabs with a rolling pin. If you have some gadgets, show how to press them gently into the clay for an incised design. If they repeat this three or four times, a pattern emerges. Have them sign their names in the slab with an ordinary lead pencil, pressing it into the clay for a good deep line. Then fire. These can be glazed or painted with tempera. Tempera is not a permanent color coat but serves the purpose if glaze is not available.

To make clay impressions, translating imagined figures or objects into dimensional clay forms, prepare the class by reading an irresistible story with a number of appealing visual images. The more vivid the child's impression, the easier it will be for him to make it in clay. Several provocative books are listed in this activity. It is a good idea to have them draw, paint, or color the images first to clarify details in two dimensions before going into three.

Old pencils, forks, spoons, and tongue depressers make good clay tools for penetrating, perforating, bonding, and decorating.

Creatures

MATERIALS
    Clay
    Nylon fishing line or heavy nylon thread for cutting clay
    Tools—pencils, tongue depressors, forks, spoons
    Water containers, preferably plastic spray

BOOKS
    Schwartz, *Kickle Snifters and Other Fearsome Critters,* illus. Glen Rounds (Lippincott).
    Mosley et al., *Crafts Design, an Illustrated Guide* (Wadsworth).
    La Mancusa, *Source Book for Art Teachers* (International Textbooks).
    Duncan and D'Amico, *How to Make Pottery and Ceramic Sculpture* (International Textbooks).

FILM
    Origin of the Species (Oregon Division of Continuing Education, Portland, Oregon).

INTERRELATING
    Language arts—using written story as motivation and writing news story as follow-up

PURPOSE
    Translate written description into a concrete form
    Interpret details and predict outcome
    Share ideas
    Invent creature experiences to fit its physical form
    Practice writing in narrative form

NEW VOCABULARY

scaly
forelegs
snorkel
zoologist
New Guinea

PROCEDURE (1–3)

Second- and third-graders who have worked with clay and made the usual sequence of pinch, slab, and coil pots are ready for a clay activity in which they make something of their own. However, many need a suggestion for getting started—something to get excited about. An imaginative and challenging set of instructions is a basic ingredient of success. Formulating such an assignment, in the arts, is a creative experience in itself.

By nature, an assignment deals with givens and guidelines, and creativity requires free play of ideas and discovery. Herein lies a dilemma, the need for a delicate balance between the two. If you pass out clay and give the assignment, "Make anything you wish," the response is likely to be less than satisfactory. Students tend to go blank with such an open invitation or to pound the clay into endless amorphous shapes, waiting for the exactly right idea, which keeps eluding them. They need some direction, some purpose to pursue.

Try giving an assignment in the form of an imaginary newspaper item, which appeared last week in the New Guinea Herald and reads like this:

CREATURE FREED

Today, just two weeks after the major earthquake in the Mamberamo River area, rumors have reached this correspondent concerning several sightings of a strange creature presumably freed from a cave in the remote Oranje Mountains by the quake.

Natives report it to be a rather scaly animal whose tracks reveal three or more toes on webbed feet. It has been eating foilage from the tops of trees, occasionally moving in an upright position using long forelegs or arms to reach out and grab plants some six feet away. It considers termites a delicacy and its nose appears of such a shape that it can probe termite mounds in search of food.

The natives report difficulty in moving close to this creature because its hearing and vision are acute, almost as if it had eyes in the back of its head. No one has been close enough to verify this fact. It can swim easily, snorkeling with this unique nose.

Concerned zoologists believe this may be a Scalamonus.

The newspaper is looking for someone who can draw or model an animal with all these characteristics. Pictures will be taken and published in the Herald so the creature can be identified and captured.

The students will, first of all, have to do some reading and translating of data. Each starts with the same descriptive elements. How they translate what they read determines the appearance of their creature.

How tall is the creature?
How many legs has it?
How long are the legs?
If it can walk upright occasionally, does it look like a human?

Are there animals that can walk upright that do not look like a human?
How many eyes does it have?
How do ears look that can pick up every sound?
How many forearms has it?
Are they definitely forearms?
What shape is its nose?
Could another shaped nose ferret termites out of a mound?
Where's New Guinea? Can you find the Oranje Mountains on a map?

All these questions are open to different interpretations except the last two.

Hopefully, 25 different Scalamani will turn up, all fulfilling the requirements. These questions give the students something to talk about while they work and the discussion should prod even the less imaginative listeners to incorporate new images in their clay creatures.

Writing a follow-up news story with the lead paragraph incorporating the who, what, when, where, and why of each student's creature and its latest exploits will push invention and drama in narrative form even further.

Group Sculptures

MATERIALS
    Clay
    Tools—tongue depressers, forks, spoons, wire thread, or nylon leader
    Water containers—bowls are fine but plastic spray containers are better

BOOKS
    Ball and Lovoos, *Making Pottery Without a Wheel*, (paperback) (Van Nostrand Reinhold).
    Cottier-Angeli, *Ceramics* (Van Nostrand Reinhold).
    Rhodes, *Clay and Glazes for the Potter* (Chilton).

FILM
    Origin of the Species (Oregon Division of Continuing Education, Portland, Oregon) Fine for grades 1–3, an excellent film.

PURPOSE
    Develop ability to work and share in group situation
    Seeking relationship of parts to the whole
    Observing and interpreting details
    Composing, recomposing, and evaluating

NEW VOCABULARY
    bisque (first firing)
    kiln
    dry foot (glazing to within ½" of bottom of piece)

PROCEDURE (1-3)

This is a group activity (three to five students in each group) that extends their abilities, to work together cooperatively. The idea is to make group animals, human figures, constructions, etcetera, by moving three-dimensional clay shapes from one person to the next for additions and modifications, until they have passed through all hands.

The groups sit at different tables. Each student in a group gets a large grapefruit-sized lump of clay. They should also have water, tongue depressers, forks, and nylon fishing line or heavy nylon thread for cutting the clay. Explain the rules first. These may be modified to fit your class, but generally they go like this:

1. In the beginning, each student starts to model with an idea in mind. It helps if you spend a few minutes talking about ideas or use a motivational approach as mentioned in Clay Impressions or Clay Creatures.
2. Every ten minutes or so each piece is passed to the student on the left.
3. The student looks at the new piece from all angles and decides what would improve it. He can continue with the original idea or alter its appearance.
4. To destroy the total shape is against the rules. There is always some area worth saving!
5. They continue working and moving the pieces until each student gets his original piece back. Count the number of people and the number of moves rather than relying on memory or the object's appearance, because it may be completely changed.
6. Each student looks carefully at what has been returned to him and asks himself what it reminds him of or how he can make it look more like what it is becoming. How can he make the shape more distinct and interesting even though it does not resemble his original? This requires of the students decision-making and the ability to change directions. As they observe what has been altered and look for ways to improve the developing form, they can learn much.

During the ten minute periods, talk about the many ways of working with clay. As the students perform various operations, write them on the board. For instance:

Clay can be added to a base as a coil or a shape.
Two shapes can be made into one, or
one can be made into several.
Clay can be perforated, combed, sliced, and stacked,
Clay can be hollowed out or cut in two
and rejoined in various ways.

How long a list can the class make? This in turn, becomes a ready reference for the student in need of a new idea.

At the end of this activity, some may question whether the pieces should be fired. Some students will regard this as just a good exercise without need for firing; others may want to keep their pieces. Making firing optional is a fair solution. After the first or bisque firing, if glaze is available, then do a second firing, have them paint it on in thin layers to the thickness of a postcard. "Dry foot" the pieces by ending the glaze coat ½" from the bottom of the piece. This prevents it from sticking to the kiln shelf.

Clay and Seeds

MATERIALS
    Clay and various tools—tongue depressors, forks, spoons, nylon fishing line for cutting
    Chia seeds.
    Several cookie sheets with sides to accommodate ¼ inch of water.

BOOKS
    Winterburn, *The Technique of Handbuilt Pottery* (Watson Guptill) (Paperback).
    Barford, *Clay in the Classroom* (Davis).
    Roettger, *Creative Clay Design* (Van Nostrand Reinhold).

INTERRELATING
    Language arts—using a story as motivation
    Science—seed germinating and growing project
    Social studies—Mexican village setting

This clay activity begins by making a clay shape, then combing some of its flat surfaces with a fork to create rough furrows. The *unglazed* piece is then fired and when cool, the furrows are planted with chia seeds. The clay shape is placed in a shallow pan of water. When the moisture reaches the surface seeds, they germinate and grow. The shape reshapes itself like magic and the entire process can be observed and discussed.

134

NEW VOCABULARY

chia seeds
furrowing
scoring

PURPOSE

Develop a tactile understanding of 3-dimensional shape through manipulation of clay
Observe a sequential transformation of a shape
Associate growth cycle of seeds with their need of light and moisture

PROCEDURE (K–3)

First experience (K–3)

Whether or not the children have worked with clay before, they should have a little time to feel and squish the clay, to squeeze and punch it in and out of shapes. This sets the stage for purposeful working. Sometimes the amorphous shapes that develop during this preliminary period will suggest animals or people. If the children have been alerted to watch for these "beings," they can elaborate on them.

Sometimes reading a story to the class, such as *Custard the Dragon (With the Big Sharp Teeth)*, gives clues to physical characteristics of dragons such as "spikes on the top of him and scales underneath, chimney for a nose and—realio, trulio daggers on his toes."* Obviously he would be even more fetching with green hair down his back, under his tummy, or between his toes. These kinds of clues help hesitant children visualize possibilities. Others need no outside help at all—dragons come naturally.

When the creature is finished to each child's satisfaction, discuss where green hair might be added, making it clear that it will not grow on vertical surfaces. Then, furrow the selected surfaces with a fork, fire the piece, and plant. Note: whenever one piece of moist clay is added to another, be sure the surfaces of both are scored.

Second experience (2—6)

Using "Sunday in the park," "Kenya on Tuesday afternoon at the watering hole," or perhaps a school football or baseball game as themes provides the students with reasons for modeling figures or animals doing things. They could work out a class sculpture with a common clay slab, furrowed and planted to accommodate the finished figures, illustrating one complete activity.

---

*Ogden Nash, *Custard the Dragon (With the Big Sharp Teeth)* (Boston: Little, Brown).

SECTION VI

Using an ELEMENT of art to integrate science and language arts

COLOR

Colorful idioms sprinkle our language. Being true blue is good. Feeling blue is bad and so is being green with envy, black-hearted, and in the red. Second-rate journalism is yellow. So is a coward.

Chasing color through history, we find that perception of it has been influenced by culture and emotion. The first recorded reference to color reveals a dependency on the practical matter of availability. The earliest colors mentioned were red and black: primitive man found red in clay soil and black in charred bones. He painted his body with them and called them magical because they were "blood" and "night." We use them as cosmetics and call them lipstick and eye liner. For centuries there was not word for blue. The ancients said something was "like the sky" until they discovered a blue mineral substance they named *lapis lazuli,* which they ground into fine dust to use as pigment. Azurite and malachite also provided blues and greens. The Phoenicians produced purple, considered rare and costly because they used the glands from thousands of murex snails to produce the tiniest amount. Only royalty could afford to buy the dye, hence, royal purple. Red, made from the dried body of the cochineal bug, was brought from Mexico to Europe by the Spanish conquistadores. And so the spectrum grew.

Theories about the use of color are many and varied but they generally agree that color is in the eye of the beholder, is influenced by the colors surrounding it, and is a highly emotional element in art and life. It must be directly experienced. No one can tell you about an exact shade of orange, you must see it. We get pleasant sensations from some colors and unpleasant sensations from others because of cultural mores, individual feelings, and, perhaps, past experience. But we can also grow to like colors we once disliked, so color, along with its effect, is very much open to conjecture.

Color can be used arbitrarily. An artist might paint a purple tree and a green sky for heightened impact. Another artist may paint the same scene in a representational way with a green tree and a blue sky. Both can evoke deeply felt emotional responses. A third way to use color is symbolically. Church and government institutions were most influential in the development of color symbolism.

In Western tradition:
> Judas is identified with a dirty yellow robe; heretics in the Middle Ages wore yellow; plague victims in the Middle Ages were identified with yellow crosses; one of the superstitions in the theater, today, is that yellow is bad luck.

In Eastern tradition:
> A bride in Israel wears yellow; yellow is sacred for a Brahman; royalty in China wore yellow.

Symbolism in color evokes a learned response.

A most important recent development in the color field is the laser beam, which is literally a beam of color capable of cutting through steel. Not only does color enhance our environment and our lives, but more and more informational and technical uses are being devised, for example, color coding in commercial and public service areas. For children, though, color is on a more elementary level. Helping them become aware of the color around them, to manipulate it, understand it, and experiment with it directly is important in the early grades.

Several of the color activities use the rainbow as a point of departure. It's a romantic and appealing subject. In Paint a Rainbow, six of the seven rainbow colors are introduced along with a simple scientific explanation of the phenomenon and its causes. Rainbow Bubbles follow. Color Variations is an elementary color mixing and comparing activity. Finger Painting is a natural medium for color mixing and for expressive line and shape.

Paint a Rainbow

MATERIALS
    Tempera or water color in red, blue, yellow
    Brushes
    Paper
    Styrofoam meat trays

BOOKS
    Lionni, *Little Blue and Little Yellow* (Astor-Honor).
    Zolotow, *Mr. Rabbit and the Lovely Present* (Harper & Row).
    O'Neill, *Hailstones and Halibut Bones* (Doubleday).
    Yolen, *Rainbow Rider* (Crowell).

INTERRELATING
    Language arts—writing a descriptive paragraph about the painting

PURPOSE
    Explore color mixing and blending

PROCEDURE (1–3)

"Bride of the rain", it's called by the North African tribe. The Italians call it "the flashing arch." Painting a rainbow is an enticing way to become acquainted with color, touch a few scientific ideas, and stimulate story telling about what happens on the other side of the rainbow.

Start with the three primary colors, blue, yellow

and red in either tempera or water color. If you are using standard paper size (8½" × 11"), cut it in half, keeping the length and reducing the width. Since the rainbow is actually a strip of seven colors bent to a half-circle, a long thin strip of paper, although flat, relates to that configuration.

Have the students paint with broad brushes, a wide red strip across the top of the paper. If they are using watercolor, keep the color intense and undiluted. Name the color. Look around the class—who is wearing red? Have the class name everything they can think of that is red. Then, they paint a wide strip of yellow right through the center of the paper. Name it. Spell it on the board. What things are yellow? Close to the bottom of the paper, they paint a wide blue strip. Repeat the naming, spelling, and color references. Introduce the word *primary* and write it on the board. Explain that other colors can be made by mixing the primaries together. Each student should have a plastic meat tray (or some container with a waterproof surface) large enough to allow for mixing fair-sized samples of color. Many children are frustrated by the small compartments in the top of the watercolor boxes provided for mixing. Have the students mix the primaries, beginning with half yellow and half red, placing them in another wide strip halfway between red and yellow on the paper. How about red and blue? They then paint this strip across the very bottom. Purple, purple, what things are purple?

In a real rainbow the colors flow together. If the students are using watercolors, they may want to run a strip of clear water between the colors, which will cause them to merge. Then again, they may wish to leave the strips as they are.

Older children can do the entire exercise by painting these strips in a half-circle on a larger sheet of paper. Encourage discussion: WHAT IS IT LIKE ON THE OTHER SIDE OF THE RAINBOW? Trade some ideas. Paint or draw them on the same paper. Some students may prefer to put themselves in the picture and record where they were the last time they saw a rainbow or where they would like to be the next time one appears. This activity can be extended to include a short paragraph about painting either fantasy or facts.

Most children know that rain and sunlight are necessary components of a rainbow. Discussion will allow them to volunteer this information. But where do the colors actually come from? Do they know that sunlight is made up of all the colors of their painted rainbows plus indigo, blue violet? If you can get a prism, hold it by the window so the sunlight passes through it and spreads the color bands like a peacock on one of the classroom walls. This is convincing evidence that each raindrop in a rainbow reflects and refracts these colors, spreading them across the sky.

Rainbow Bubbles

MATERIALS
- Liquid detergent
- Glycerin
- Styrofoam cups
- Straws
- Shallow pans

BOOKS
- Lamorisse, *The Red Balloon* (Doubleday).
- Mayer, *Bubble Bubble* (Parents Magazine Press).

INTERRELATING
- Science—investigating the contention that warm air rises, and the spectrum of colors making a rainbow

PURPOSE
Experimenting and demonstrating theories:
- how to blow the largest bubble
- how to combine bubbles
- how to hold the pipe for best results
- why they fly up and not down

PROCEDURE (K-2)

An activity using the rainbow as its theme is the blowing of huge rainbow-mirror bubbles. For young children—kindergartners and first-graders—watching them float up, up, and away is irresistible magic, and the surface color patterns reflect the colors of the spectrum. Blowing bubbles outside on a sunny day is particularly effective, especially if you accompany the activity with questions and comments. NAME THE COLORS YOU SEE ON THE BUBBLE. ARE ALL THE COLORS OF THE RAINBOW PRESENT? WHAT ELSE DO YOU SEE REFLECTED ON THE SURFACE? WHAT ELSE CAN YOU NAME THAT REFLECTS OBJECTS? WHY DOES THE BUBBLE FLOAT UP? Working a little science into the project, have them blow their hands and ask if their breath is warm or cold. THEN, IS THE AIR INSIDE THE BUBBLE WARM OR COLD? COULD IT BE THAT THE WARM AIR LIFTS BUBBLES? WHAT ELSE CAN YOU NAME THAT IS ROUND, FULL OF AIR, AND FLOATS? HOW LARGE CAN YOU MAKE A BUBBLE? IF YOU STAND CLOSE TO SOMEONE ELSE BLOWING A BUBBLE, CAN YOU COMBINE THE TWO WITHOUT BREAKING EITHER? DID YOU KNOW THAT A BUBBLE WALL IS 5,000 TIMES THINNER THAN ONE HAIR ON YOUR HEAD? There will be much conversation accompanied by chasing of bubbles and squealing. Doing this outside gives the children a sense of freedom. Also, when the bubble formula drips, it won't matter.

The formula is simple: two cups of water, ¼ cup liquid detergent, and ¼ cup glycerin. It's failsafe. The bubble pipe is made from a Styrofoam cup with a hole punched in the side about midway between top and bottom, through which a straw is inserted halfway into the cup. CAREFULLY DIP THE RIM OF THE CUP INTO THE FORMULA UNTIL A BUBBLE OR SHEET OF THE FORMULA COVERS THE OPENING. Then blow gently through the straw, making a huge bubble. A slight flick of the wrist releases the bubble into the air.

To eliminate wasteful spilling, pour the formula into several shallow pans to a depth of ½" and place them on the ground. Allow for five to eight children to a pan.

Reading *Bubble Bubble* by Mercer Mayer either before or after bubbling fits nicely into the spirit of the activity.

Color Variations

MATERIALS
    Tempera or water color—red, blue, yellow, white, and black
    Brushes
    Paper

BOOKS
    Tison and Taylor, *The Adventures of the Three Colors* (World Publishing).
    Polendori, *Color* (*Stepping into Science Series*) (Children's Press).
    Wolff, *Seeing Red* (Scribner's).

PURPOSE
    Refine the color sense
    Develop ability to differentiate between tints and shades of one color
    Consider potential color variations

PROCEDURE (2-3)

    Early in the children's painting experience, try this short activity that has meaning for children just becoming consciously aware of color. Unless the variation of a single color is brought to their attention, they tend to use the colors just as they come from the paint box or tempera jar. As a preliminary to the following color experimentation, have the class look around the room and pick out all the blues, yellows, or reds they can find. They will find many of the blues on clothing. Have the students wearing these blues stand together to point out the variations of shades.

Pass out paint—the three primary colors plus white. The task is to mix blue and white in varying amounts to make as many blue shades as possible. A great deal of paint will be saved if you suggest they start with white and add blue. Pass a piece of paper on which you have drawn a 2" grid among groups of six children and have each child put down one or two blues mixed with white. The game is for each to add a slightly different tint than any on the page. When this is completed, give each child some black. In this case, start with the blue and add the black a little at a time. Pass a second piece of paper and record the findings. Display these when dry so all can see how many different tints and shades can be made just by adding white or black to a color. Do the same with the other two primary colors. Working with yellow is particularly fascinating because it turns a shade of green when black is added. They will be surprised and intrigued.

When the displays are taken down, have the students cut them up and arrange them in a row, from the lightest to the darkest color. This is an excellent exercise in color perception.

Finger Painting

MATERIALS
> Powdered or dry tempera paint, or commercial finger paint
> Starch
> Shelf paper, butcher paper, or finger paint paper
> Newspapers
> Pan for water
> Sponge
> Spoon

BOOKS
> Scott, *Finger Painting* (London: Batsford).

PURPOSE
> Direct involvement with paint and color
> Experimentation with movement of line and shape
> Exploration of color blending
> Composing and designing

PROCEDURE (K–3)

Finger painting is a direct and natural technique. After all, fingers came before brushes, and getting into the paint, feeling the texture, and watching the flow is irresistible for most children. The technique allows them to move and change images as quickly as ideas come. Initial success is invariable. These facts make a strong case for introducing finger painting early and doing it often.

This is a messy kind of painting so it's good to set aside an area close to the sink, easily cleaned up, where one or two children can work at a time. Finger painting is

145

not the best activity for full class participation. The working surface should be as large as possible; a formica table, a plastic-covered area, or a piece of glossy hardboard. The student should stand while he paints, wearing an apron or an old shirt buttoned up the back. He should roll up his sleeves. Give each child a pan of water, a spoon, and a sponge. A short demonstration by you showing how much paint to spoon onto the surface and the beginning movements of the hand, arm, and fingers, is about all that is needed. Start with one color and work up to three. It may take several sessions for some children to move from hesitant gestures to large, easy movements.

Direct Process

Begin by covering the work area with newspapers. Dip a sheet of finger painting paper or shelf paper into a pan of water and place it on the newspapers, glossy side up. Put four teaspoons of starch in the center and sprinkle some dry or liquid tempera on top. Distribute this over the entire surface with both hands. Use the finger tips, fists, side of the hands, arm, elbow, one finger, two fingers, the thumb and little finger, then all five, then ten. Even simple hand prints make interesting prints in the beginning. When the picture is finished, lift it by the corners and lay it out to dry on newspapers. The paintings will want to curl, so as soon as they're dry, stack them and weight them with books for a day or overnight.

Indirect Process

If a formica table or glossy hardboard is used as a base for painting instead of paper, proceed as above with starch and paint. When the child has created a painting he particularly likes, have him wash his hands, take a piece of newsprint, and "pull a proof" by placing the paper over the design and smoothing it down with his hands, ever so gently. Peel the paper off and he has a monoprint. Clean the surface of the table or hardboard and it's ready for the next painting.

To sustain interest after several sessions, ease into color mixing. If the child is working with yellow (always start with the lightest color and add the darker—it's more economical), blue may be introduced a little at a time into the yellow. All shades of green develop as mixing progresses. Have him start with yellow again and add red. Then start with red and add blue. Then mix all three for brown.

Smooth-surface linoleum squares may be substituted for hardboard and a commercial finger paint may be substituted for starch and tempera.

SECTION VII
Management

Evaluations

Evaluation in the arts is a ticklish business for both the teacher and the student. How does one measure individuality? We say the arts encourage divergent thinking and doing, that they stimulate innovation and overall originality. To compare one student with another is not to encourage this individuality. To set a general standard against which to measure performance is a contradiction. Yet the teacher has a responsibility for making constructive comments to encourage the student to build his own mechanism for judgment, to develop a critical awareness of what he is doing.

One constructive method of evaluation that does not compromise individuality is to compare the student's most recent work with his earlier efforts. He becomes his own competition. On a regular basis, perhaps during an art session, talk, on a one-to-one basis, with two or three children successively while the others are working. With each child, compare a current painting or drawing with several older ones. Discuss the similarities and differences. Is his use of color expanding? Is he considering the size of his paper in relation to the size of the objects drawn? Is he observing more carefully and translating his observation into his work? Is there something he would like to try? The child may laugh at his inept paintings from the beginning of the year, but this indicates growth. The child's course of development is not linear and therefore not always easy to discern. The zigzag pattern of artistic development makes an occasional overview highly profitable.

Reviewing work also exposes any repetitious use of symbols and colors. A child might repeat a shape, a color relationship, or a technique several times after he has learned it because he enjoys it and wishes to secure it in his art vocabulary. But if this repetition goes on for a month or two, assuming he has drawn or painted several times a week, then the child is imitating himself. This is a danger signal: he is in a rut and needs fresh motivation or new material.

Evaluation is really unnecessary as long as the kindergarten or first-grade child is working freely and effectively in art. When he becomes hesitant or dissatisfied with his work, often around the second or third grade, he is looking for assistance. This child probably has been exposed to a daily diet of visual materials on television over a period of years. He knows how things should look and if he is unable to produce the image he has in mind with any degree of proficiency, he becomes frustrated. Unless he has had regular art experience during his school career, in which he converted his inner images through materials into some kind of acceptable statement, then theory has outstripped performance and this, according to Leonardo da Vinci, is the supreme misfortune. His mental image of how it should be has become far more precise than his ability to express it. The two should have been developing together. If the gap between them is allowed to widen, by junior high or the middle grades his lack of ability mixes with his ego and he stops drawing rather than expose his incompetence to peers.

Another approach to evaluating is to structure the art lesson so that opportunities for innovation will occur in the course of fulfilling specific requirements. These requirements motivate the child to get into the activity. Once he is involved, the material and the excitement of exploration will likely carry him far beyond the basic requirements into inventive variations of his own. For an example, see Clay Creatures.

Another example is a graphics lesson using gadget printing. Set out a collection of objects that easily print a clear image: keys, spring clothespins, small combs, washers, etcetera. Make a stamp pad, as outlined in Pattern on Pattern. Write the following requirements on the chalkboard:

1. Print one of the shapes in one color at least ten times on a piece of newsprint. In this way the student gets the feel of the process, how much ink or paint to use, and how much pressure to apply. Random printing allows him complete freedom to master the mechanics.
2. Print the same shape in one color at least ten times in a pattern you invent on a second sheet of paper.
   If you have not introduced pattern to the class, this is an excellent time because in graphic technique any shape can be printed repeatedly. This emphasizes the factor of repetition, which is basic to patterning. If the class has worked in pattern before, this reinforces the concept.
3. Print this shape and a second shape in a pattern using two colors.

The child is progressing, step by step, into more complex patterning and color usage.
4. Try overlap if you wish.

Overlap uncovers a whole new world of possibilities. We are at the point where the children have experienced printing, patterning, combining colors, and overlapping shape and color. The stage is set for all kinds of performances.

Depending on class conduct in an open situation, and individual capabilities and interest, the extension of this activity can take at least three directions. First, continue in a structured way by varying the colored background paper—print on paper toweling, tissue, patterned wrapping paper, and on old sheeting to make head bands or scarves. Second, set up a variety of papers and colored paints on a table or counter top, where, on completion of desk work, one or two students may experiment with design and printing. Or third, open up the activity and let the class continue to work on its own, introducing new kinds of paper and additional paint colors as motivation. Let the ideas roll. Hold up any innovative ones for the whole class to see and they will generate other ideas.

Occasional suggestions can renew children's energy and enthusiasm. For instance, they may wish to try partners and combine shapes for printing. A total class project can be done concurrently with the individual work and partner printing. Place a piece of butcher paper on the floor, preferably on a cushion of newspapers for better printing. Announce that all members of the class can print on it at teacher-directed intervals, or as the mood strikes them, or depending on class demeanor and enthusiasm at the time.

Bringing organization to the random printing that will first occur is a genuine learning experience. Draw ideas from the children. Talk about relating the stamped prints through movement, color grouping, or color contrasting. Concentrate an assortment of stamps in one area as a focal point and surround them with a clear space; or stamp the prints within an outline of a flower or animal shape.

Discussions about classroom displays present an excellent opportunity for the students to develop their evaluating talents. These "seminars" need not be long, but they should be frequent. Five minutes of solid, perceptive conversation at regular intervals, two or three times a week, can do wonders. Frequent observations and discussions refine the student's aptitude for judgment. Their tolerance for repetitive clichéd work diminishes, and they learn to value inventive ideas. As they share their responses, each child practices verbalizing thoughts and feelings and increases his visual awareness. Since there are no absolutes in art and much of it is subjective, a consensus gained through informal dialogue can reveal a credible perspective.

Conducting such discussions at the beginning of the art session gets the ideas flowing. The child immediately follows this with painting, drawing, collaging, or printing, thus trying what has been talked about before it becomes diluted or forgotten.

Discussions and observations serve another purpose. The first- to third-grade child may never progress beyond his charming kindergarten drawings of figures and animals unless he is urged to observe figures and animals as a preliminary exercise to drawing them, as mentioned in the section About Perceiving. The longer he clings to his own shorthand versions of objects, the more difficult he finds it to break the habit of substituting them for carefully observed ones.

Every creative move the student makes is based on selecting and evaluating. Perhaps it makes more sense to say that every move is based on evaluating, then selecting. Either way, practice—trial and error—brings selecting and evaluating closer together, until they become a single action and the child is at once artist and critic. The intrinsic value of these processes is significant for each child whether or not he shows a particular aptitude for the arts. This is dealt with at length in The Additional Benefits of Learning Through the Arts.

Exhibitions

A drawing, painting, collage, or any kind of art work takes on a whole new perspective when it is moved from desk top or easel to the wall. A little distancing makes for clearer judgment. There is some truth in the old hackneyed film portrayal of an artist by John Barrymore, who, to be convincing, painted a bit then stepped way back from his canvas, tilted his head to one side then the other, squinted his eyes, and looked critically at his work. In the classroom, putting a little distance between the child and his collage by displaying it on a bulletin board allows him to step back and look at it with a fresh perspective.

Suppose an exhibition of class drawings is tacked up on the wall. When the class looks at 25 individual interpretations of a single subject such as a couple of students posing, several trees in the school yard, or a visiting rabbit complete with cage, any unique qualities will become obvious. One child may draw his rabbit with heavy, bold lines that can be seen across the room. A second child may use fine, light lines requiring the viewer to move in very close. Students, with a brief guided discussion, come to see that light pencil lines convey an impression of a soft, furry, delicate animal, and heavy lines can call attention to the strength and power of movement inherent in the rabbit. A drawing is an individual interpretation of what one sees and wishes to say, visually, about the object he is drawing. The student can store away information about line quality and what it communicates for future recall. When he wishes to suggest something soft and furry, he will remember to try light pencil lines; when drawing the trunk of a tree or the profile of a mountain, he will remember that heavy thick lines look powerful and strong.

One child may draw a tiny rabbit on a large world of paper while another bumps both edges with his drawing. Spacing, size, and line elements are all obvious here, and not at all difficult for the class to observe and talk about. Each child sees, feels, and knows through his own experience. Sharing a variety of responses to works in art broadens his insights.

Second- and third-grade children drawing from a real object tend to concentrate all their interest on the object in isolation. The day someone suggests a background for a drawing can be the day everyone becomes aware that objects have environments. Use the opportunity to examine whether anything exists alone in space. Must everything in the background be included or just those shapes, colors or lines that enhance the drawing? There is poetic license and artistic license and unless the teacher specifically requires all the detail in the background, the student-artist should be free to select from the visual hash around him only what he wishes to use. The good cook never puts all the kitchen spices into one dish; rather he selects those that deliver the clearest, most tantalizing flavor. It is the same with drawing or painting.

From the second grade on, let the children, in small committees, hang their own exhibitions, even if it amounts to only four or five items. It is helpful if a definite space is provided. They can learn to use thumb tacks and masking tape. Since they will hang work only as high as they can reach—lower than is customary in most classrooms—it will have the psychological effect of making the display their own. Over a period of time they should become sensitive to the fact that paintings and drawings hanging side by side can complement or interfere with each other. This can be brought to their attention during discussion periods with a question or two: DO SOME PAINTINGS WHISPER WHILE OTHERS SHOUT? IS IT BEST TO GROUP THESE? (Hanging pictures in a related cluster is a form of visual categorization that makes then easier to see and appreciate.) DOES THE AMOUNT OF SPACE BETWEEN THEM MAKE A DIFFERENCE? ARE THEY EASIER TO SEE IF HUNG CLOSE TOGETHER OR IF GIVEN BREATHING SPACE? Aligning tops or sides of paintings and keeping the spaces separating them consistent establishes a sense of order, but it must be experienced to be understood. This procedure can be used occasionally to draw out the children's opinions about how ordered and random hanging compare.

Matting always makes a picture look better. A picture, person, place, or thing, when separated from its environment and considered singly, is simply easier to see. A mat also gives any work a finished look. Have the children mat a few of their paintings and drawings and decide for themselves if the mat makes a difference.

Many magazine ads are excellent examples of isolating for emphasis—they surround a colorful item with the passivity and contrast of white space. Bring in examples and compare them with ads that bury the sales item in color, line, and copy; this makes a good case. Have a game of it. Ask which product makes the most immediate impression? Why? Using examples from the "real world" helps the students find the concepts they are learning in practical usage.

The simplest mat is made by glueing the art work onto a larger piece of construction paper. There are two rules to remember: the amount of mat showing below the drawing should be wider than the amount at top, and the drawing should be equidistant from either side of the mat.

Using cardboard boxes is another effective way to display art works. A common gift box provides two shadow frames. Cover the bottom of the box, inside, with colored construction paper and mount the drawing on top with thumb tacks, which in turn hold the painting, colored paper, and box on the wall. Deep boxes can be used for three-dimensional work. For variation, thumb tack a box bottom to the wall, put the lid on, and mount the drawing on the top of the lid for a raised instead of recessed effect. A grouping of five or six makes an attractive, reusable display.

Colored mats are exciting to use. Sometimes a colored mat picks up a color from the work and gives the original more punch. However, a bright color may attract all the attention and force the painting to become a secondary interest. A rainy-day scene may have more impact with a blue mat than a red one, whereas a delicate line drawing can be overwhelmed by the same blue mat. The color and size of the mat should be in keeping with the feeling and tonality of the painting, drawing, or collage; the best way to learn this is through experimentation and observation.

Hanging things from the ceiling is an effective and lively way to display. Like sculpture, whatever is hung will be seen from all directions. This presents a whole new rationale for creating three-dimensional art and could be the basis of several projects. It is a natural lead-in to suspended objects such as mobiles, cut-paper constructions, and ceramic shapes fired and strung on a thin rope like beads. These types of displays give a room a more intimate atmosphere and a visual lift. Hang work in the halls, the library, the principal's office, and the cafeteria. Student work brings life to bare walls.

Occasionally invite the children to bring to school a piece of "art" they particularly like. Have a class display, make a big thing of it. Third-graders are natural collectors anyway. The children can arrange the contributions in group exhibits. Again, take time to talk about these treasures. If this is done five or six times a year, the kinds of things brought in will give the teacher clues about what art means to each child and reveal how, if at all, their choices have been influenced by their experiences with art in the classroom (and which are most effective). This activity may also suggest areas needing exploration like design, color, or texture. Who knows what can be learned?

Involving Parents

Children's enthusiam for the arts is great. To sustain this love affair, parental encouragement and support is extremely important. The child in the early elementary grades reflects family attitudes and influences. Parental reaction, outwardly expressed and/or inwardly felt by the child sets a strong model.

Parents want the best for their children. Why not let this work for the arts program? A letter sent home at the beginning of the year is a positive start. A general outline of the program and some of the philosophy behind it lets parents feel part of their child's education. Most parents will welcome a short, clearly stated rationale and some guidelines. Many have little background in the arts and want to respond affirmatively to their child's work but are unsure of the form it should take. Many more simply do not know how the arts can benefit their child's development as a whole, functioning human being. Finally, living in a visually oriented culture with constant exposure to television, picture magazines, and films, children need training in the visual arts to become intelligent and discriminating observers. What they are seeing affects their process of learning.

It's the nature of parents to see their children as special. Therefore, they will welcome the considerable emphasis on individual growth and expression that is basic to the arts.

The parents should know that every child has the ability to think and do things creatively, but that it must be supported and guided. The creative ability must have time to germinate and produce; this requires a warm, accepting atmosphere and encouragement from both teacher and parent.

The young child is extremely imaginative and will make shapes and colors and squiggles and dots that have real meaning for him, even though they may not look like much to the rest of us. But then, child art is not adult art and no one would want it to be. This is why the art teacher doesn't need to show the child how to draw or how something is supposed to look, but instead sets up circumstances in which the child can learn to draw for himself, feeling the satisfaction and fulfillment that result from independent accomplishment.

Looking at the work the child brings home, the parents can talk about an exciting use of color or a shape that draws their attention, rather than asking the child to identify the shapes and colors as a particular "something" the parents can recognize. If the child is inclined to talk about the work, the parents should encourage him to do so. Then again, he may say nothing. Art is visual and words are verbal—they are two distinct languages. If the child could tell all about how he feels and sees and knows, he would have no motivation to paint it.

One of the greatest compliments a parent can pay a child is to look at each piece of work he brings home, whether it is math, English, social studies, or art. By hanging a drawing or painting, he tells the child that he values the work.

Supplying materials for use at home is positive reinforcement parents can make. These need not be expensive. Any kind of plain paper—construction, wrapping, or typewriter—together with felt-tip pens, tempera paint, and wide brushes are fine for starters. The cheap 1" nylon sash brushes from the hardware store work well. With these tools, the child can practice drawing and painting large shapes and colored lines, and learn eye-hand coordination while developing small and large muscle coordination. Other good home materials are clay and crayons.

Something should be said about the use of coloring books: they will cripple, if not destroy, the child's creative spark at an early age. There is little or no educational value in them. Many coloring books claim to teach history or geography along with art by having children color maps, costumes from other cultures, and even cultural motifs. No research exists to prove that the child learns anything more than to color within the lines, someone else's line. Coloring books deny every quality in the child that good education in the arts tries to nurture. The child learns no skill through coloring dittos or coloring books that he could not better understand through the simplest original activity. Even if the child colors beautifully, he can hardly feel a sense of achievement because the product is not entirely his. Coloring books are busy work, a mindless, directionless activity.

Some parents need a little help in defining just what a "creative art activity" might be. Sending home an occasional outline with a list of easily collected materials for such activities may be just the incentive they need. A reference to this approach to home involvement is included in the following letter, which was actually used at the kindergarten level.

Dear Parent:

Making art is an experience of joy and an act of communication for your kindergarten child. Since his speaking and writing vocabulary is limited, he draws what he thinks and feels. Art is a visual language, a language of thoughts and feelings spoken through line, color and shape.

Kindergarten is a wonder world of new experiences. Just learning to use a brush, to cut with scissors or to paste colors on paper is an adventure and a learning experience. The child is becoming a thoughtful observer and doer. He is getting to know himself and his environment better. As he clarifies his eye-mind-hand coordination and refines his observation skills, he is building readiness for reading.

At this age he needs acceptance and support from his parents and teachers. Why not put some of his art work up at home? He will feel appreciated and capable. Sometimes his paintings will include recognizable objects. Sometimes they will just be arrangements of shapes and colors because he is experimenting with brushes and paint and learning to compose and organize. Whether his work portrays recognizable objects or abstract colors and shapes, both are acceptable as art and necessary for his development. We don't expect our children to talk, behave or think like adults. Neither should we expect them to draw like adults. The child's view is very different from ours and while his drawings may look strange to us they are very real to him. Probing, exploring and investigating in his own way at his own rate of speed is essential for his growth.

Children love working with art materials but if the child is "dressed up" he may hesitate to become involved. This can deprive him of a valuable experience because every picture a child draws or paints is a step in his development. He will feel free and uninhibited if he is wearing play clothes or an old shirt of his father's.

Providing some simple materials for your child to work with at home like felt-tip pens, crayons, any kind of plain paper, children's scissors, brushes, paint, construction paper, paste and magazines for collage are great confidence builders. Covering a table top and surrounding floor with newspapers which can be rolled up and thrown away when the child has finished saves cleanup time.

Modeling and constructing are valuable activities. Play dough is a fine material to use and can be stored in the refrigerator for use over a period of time. A good recipe is included as well as a list of everyday things to collect for a fascinating "junk box". Each month we will send home directions for an activity using this junk material. These activities are designed to stimulate creativity and are much to be preferred to coloring books which stifle individual expression in short order.

Why not try making some "art" with your child using your collected materials?

Sincerely yours,
The Kindergarten Staff

In districts with bilingual classrooms, this letter can be translated into the appropriate language.

Play Dough Recipe
4 cups flour
1 cup salt
1½ cups water
2 tablespoons tempera if color is desired
Mix thoroughly.

Junk Box Contributions

milk carton	bones	sponges
cloth scraps	feathers	stockings
costume jewelry	rice/macaroni/	cord
innertubes	beans (dried)	chains
marbles	buttons	mirrors
tape	buckles	wrapping paper
tubes	bracelets	phonograph
egg cartons	boxes	records
photographs	juice cans	beads
magazines	tuna fish cans	wood scraps
pine cones	eyeglass frames	cardboard
pipe cleaners	game cards	spools
yarn	dowels	sandpaper
wallpaper	shoelaces	bricks
clothes pins	contact paper	tongue depressors
straws	Styrofoam meat	tiles or linoleum
envelopes	trays	bottle caps
paper bags		

Afterword

Why is exposure to the arts important for the child or for any of us? Because the arts encourage us to dream, to imagine possibilities outside and beyond ourselves. How do we think a new thought or see a new vision except through imagination and intuition? Einstein considered imagination more valuable than knowledge.

The arts are also important because they provide concrete experiences in which we manipulate physical materials by ordering, categorizing, constructing, and interpreting symbols and shapes. To acquire cognitive skills and express himself, the child "must 'play out' what he thinks and symbolize his ideas by means of gestures or objects, and represent things by imitation, drawing and construction," according to Jean Piaget. In the arts, the child must organize his own symbols and shapes and this teaches him to think and feel. Without this kind of practice the student is forced to operate through stereotypes and prejudices, often out of ignorance rather than intent.

It has been said that persistence will finally yield us knowledge but imagination must be pursued and courted. Creative exploration is chancy, it's risky, it's sometimes frustrating because it requires traveling in strange territory. But when we reach a clear new insight, even for a moment, we know we've touched something profound and unique. It's an act of recreating, of re-humanizing ourselves—as the arts heighten the quality of our lives and intensify our experiences. In this book we have talked much about the visual arts, somewhat about movement and dance, music and mime, and even included a small measure of poetry.

In choosing one of the arts to make a final statement for them all, let's consider poetry—how it relates to life and values—by reading a short verse from William Carlos Williams's poem, *Asphodel, That Greeny Flower**:

>   it is difficult
>   to get the news from poems
>   yet men die miserably every day
>   for lack of
>   what is found there.

News comes in many forms; good tidings, disasters, advice, substantial information, inspiring ideas, rumor, and scandal. Both television and daily papers present a bewildering array of random happenings, having only currency in common. Brevity is the goal, often practiced at the expense of clarity, and we are presented with isolated events without background or follow-up. We experience no *before,* no *after,* only a relentless, fragmented *now.* We are galvanized by short shocks and incomplete impressions, which makes us hard on the surface and uncertain within.

In poetry (or painting or drama or music), on the other hand, such diversified information and experience is examined and retained only if it contributes to a pattern of meaning, responding to the basic concerns *in* life, not merely *about* life. The poet arranges his tough/tender insights in order to make them comprehensible to the reader—the reader, that is, who wants to understand. So it is with the arts, which speak of hope and compassion, of wholeness and joy, and prove that these are present and possible.

---

* *Pictures from Brueghel and Other Poems.* Copyright 1954 by William Carlos Williams. Reprinted by permission of New Directions.